Wilts Baydon

What constitutes a church?

The English Church free from the errors of the Churches of Rome and of

Germany

Wilts Baydon

What constitutes a church?
The English Church free from the errors of the Churches of Rome and of Germany

ISBN/EAN: 9783337112813

Printed in Europe, USA, Canada, Australia, Japan

Cover: Foto ©Lupo / pixelio.de

More available books at **www.hansebooks.com**

WHAT CONSTITUTES A CHURCH?

OR,

The English Church

FREE FROM THE ERRORS OF THE CHURCHES OF ROME

AND GERMANY;

TOGETHER WITH

LETTERS TO THE REV. LORD SIDNEY G. OSBORNE,

ON HIS REMARKS ON THE BISHOP OF SALISBURY'S CHARGE;

AND TO

THE CHURCHWARDENS OF THE DIOCESE OF SARUM.

BY

J. A. WILLIAMS,

ONE OF THE CHURCHWARDENS OF BAYDON, NORTH WILTS.

London,

RIVINGTONS, WATERLOO PLACE;

HIGH STREET, | TRINITY STREET,
Oxford. | Cambridge.

1867.

TO THE

RIGHT REV. THE LORD BISHOP OF SALISBURY.

My Lord,

The letters on the Christian Church, included in this pamphlet, which I take the liberty of dedicating to your Lordship, were written, the most of them, before the delivery of your Charge at your recent Visitation.

As, unhappily, there has been through your diocese an opinion, among too many, that the contents of your Charge are not in harmony with the principles of the Reformed English Church,—the Rev. Lord Sidney G. Osborne, too, having published in the *Times* a letter, intimating that you ought no longer to remain within her pale—and the "Anti-Ritualistic" meeting held at Salisbury, to condemn the principles you advocate—induce me, although the letters were signed "A Churchwarden of North Wilts," to acknowledge the authorship, and give them publicity, in the hope that many who may read them will go through the Bible as I have done, and see for themselves the order and discipline that the Almighty requires in His Universal Church, and contrast it with the bitter feelings that have existed in our own Church since the Reformation.

The letters to Lord Sidney G. Osborne and the Churchwardens of your diocese, were written with a view to counteract what I consider a breach of that decorum in those whose duty it is *to learn*, rather than *to teach*; and as your Lord-

2.

ship is entrusted with the *great responsibility of teaching*, not only the Clergy, but the Laity through them, I tender you my humble thanks for the manly and straightforward manner in which you have done so in your Charge.

Hoping, and offering my prayers, that you might be spared for many years to come, that you may witness the fruits of your labour,

I beg to subscribe myself

Your Lordship's faithful Servant

and Churchwarden,

J. A. WILLIAMS.

BAYDON, NORTH WILTS,
  Nov. 4, 1867.

PREFACE.

The following letters on "The Christian Church," published in the early part of the present year in the *Devizes Gazette*, and signed "A Churchwarden of North Wilts," were called forth on account of that paper being filled, week after week, with meetings of different societies, at which Clergymen of the Church of England scrupled not to deny the spiritual office they held; with letters, too, from some few individuals denouncing our Bishop's principles as Romanistic, and an address from a large number of influential farmers in the county, *thanking* the Rev. Lord Sidney G. Osborne for the part he had taken against the Bishop.

In offering them to the public, I am free to confess myself the author. There was no need for this whilst writing them; but as, on reading the letter of S. G. O. commenting on the Bishop's Charge, and having it sent me *as a Churchwarden*, with a request to assist in remonstrating against the said Charge—having *heard* it throughout, and being satisfied that our Church in her Articles and Service *taught* what the Bishop had declared, I felt constrained to write the letter (which will be found in the Appendix) to the Rev. Lord, and also felt bound to acknowledge myself the author of the other letters.

The proofs I have given of "What constitutes a Church?"

are mainly quotations from the Scriptures, and I would earnestly and respectfully ask my readers to do, as the Bereans of old did—to search them, and see "*whether these things are so;*" and I trust, by God's providence, a more united feeling may exist within the Church, on so sacred and vital a part of our religion.

J. A. WILLIAMS.

BAYDON, NORTH WILTS,
July 15, 1867.

WHAT CONSTITUTES A CHURCH?

LETTER I.

To the Editor of the "Devizes Gazette."

DEAR SIR,—Your columns have of late contained a variety of
theological discussion and opinion, which has no doubt been read
with much interest, and, in my case, with no small amount of
sorrow and concern for the welfare of our Church. We have seen,
in two instances (Devizes and Calne), Clergymen from Bristol
and London attending a public meeting and declaring "*they were
no Priests*"—although THEY had solicited their respective Bishops
to admit them to Priest's Orders, and had received from them the
authority, "Receive the Holy Ghost for the office and work of a
Priest in the Church of God, *now committed unto thee* by the imposition of our hands. Whose sins thou dost forgive, they are
forgiven; and whose sins thou dost retain, they are retained. And
be thou a faithful dispenser of the Word of God, and of His Holy
Sacraments: in the name of the Father, and of the Son, and of
the Holy Ghost." This office was solicited by the two individuals
above mentioned, and (I blush while I write it) they have *denied
the efficacy* of the holy office they have undertaken. Your corre-
spondent, too, from East Kennett—*another Clergyman*—seems to
me to be vainly attempting to prove the same thing. Then we
have a gentleman from Avebury *professing to belong to the Church
of England*, but denying her authority, and establishing a FREE
CHURCH in that parish, forgetting that "*Unity is strength.*" He
has been filling your columns for the past twelve months. Next
we have the "Church Union" meeting at Devizes (would that it
were *an Union*) attempting to show us the necessity of high
ritualism; and then the Rev. Lord S. G. O., writing of *our* Bishop
in terms which seem to me not very becoming towards a supe-
rior. The Bishop's mild and Christian reply, too; and lastly, the
address of seventy-five of our Wiltshire farmers to the Rev. Lord
S. G. O., thanking him for the part he had taken *against their own
Bishop.*

Surely, Mr. Editor, there must be something wrong in the
teaching of our Church, that all these several parties *can fancy*

themselves to be right, and professing to belong to the same Church, the very doctrine of which, as laid down by our Saviour Himself, is, "Be ye all *as one,* even as my Father and I are one."

I have been looking for years past to find out the cause of this miserable division of opinion in our Church, and I have no hesitation in saying that it can be traced back to the glorious Reformation. I do not deny that it was a glorious Reformation, as it cleansed the English Church from the errors and heresies of the Church of Rome ; but, at the same time, it was shorn of the greater part of its glory, by introducing into our Church those divisions which have existed from that time to the present, and are now getting *too hot* long to remain as they have been. It, therefore, behoves every man who has the interest and welfare of his Church at heart, to put a spoke in the wheel, and aid in maintaining her in righteousness and truth !

With this motive in view (with your permission) I will attempt to show what, after much study, I am satisfied are the true principles of the English Church ; and, that I may not be deemed egotistical or puffed up in my own opinion, I "will show the reason why ! !"

There are two parties in our Church, termed the High and the Low Church ; and I trust there are a vast number, myself among them, who are content to be called CHURCHMEN ; viz., those who take the Prayer Book, agree to all they see therein, as taught by our forefathers ; and who, after saying the three Creeds as they come in order, *actually believe* what they say they do ; and in partaking of the *two* Holy Sacraments, believe them to be what the Fathers of the Church and our Saviour Himself say they are !

Thus prefacing, my subject shall be entitled, "The Principles and Faith of the English Church, apart from the Errors of the Church of Rome on the one hand, and the Churches of Germany on the other!"

There is such a thing as *consistency,* and in nothing is it so necessary that it should develop itself as in Ecclesiastical matters. We will see how this material is welded into the principles of those who have been so prominent in causing the controversy that has arisen amongst us, and which eventually will cause the *serious* members of our Church who differ, to consider, whether it is not possible that they may be wrong in the opinions they have imbibed from their youth. It is very certain that *all* cannot be right ; and I am free to confess for myself, that in holding the opinions I do now, they are totally different from what I held in my youth. A simple narrative of facts as they occurred will illustrate my case. As a young married man, I held to the doctrine of the *Low Church* —viz., I did not believe in regeneration in baptism ; and I understood but little of the other Sacrament, further than, as a member of the Church, to do as I was bid. The Oxford controversy was going on, but not a single tract have I ever seen. I was quite satisfied to condemn the whole of those who were termed High Church ; but a curious circumstance occurred. Dr. Pusey was to preach before the University; and his subject was, "The Real Presence in the Sacrament of the Lord's Supper." I thought it must be heresy, that it could be nothing more or less than the doctrine of Transubstantiation; and so, I suppose, thought some of the authorities at Oxford—for his sermon was demanded, and, *without any cause assigned*, it was pronounced heretical, and he was prohibited from preaching again for three years. Dr. Pusey demanded that they should show in what part of the sermon the heresy consisted; but this the authorities *declined doing*, and I said to myself, however I may differ from Dr. Pusey, this conduct of the Oxford men *is not* CONSISTENT; it was like the case of St. Paul, when Festus told Agrippa "that it seemed to him *unreasonable* to send a prisoner, and not withal to *signify* the crimes laid against him." The sermon being published, I got a copy; it seemed mystical at first sight; but, after reading it three times, I had reason to thank God for the light given me. It showed plainly what the English Church held. He quoted some of the best of the early writers, as Hooker, George Herbert, &c., and he summed up by quoting our Saviour's own words, "Take, eat, *this is my body;*" and he observed, "*He said it, and I believe it.*" But he proved it to be there in a *spiritual* sense, and not *carnally*, as the Romish Church hath it. I felt convinced that I had been wrong, but I determined to look further. I knew that Ridley had been a martyr for this very cause; so, having his life, I looked to see what he said on the matter, and to my satisfaction I read as follows:—When asked by the Bishop of Lincoln to show what were his opinions of Christ's presence in the Sacrament, he answered, "Both you and I agree that in the Sacrament is the very true and natural body and blood of Christ, even that which was born of the Virgin Mary, which ascended into heaven, which sitteth at the right hand of God the Father, which shall come from thence to judge the quick and the dead; only we differ *in modo, in the way and manner* of being; we confess all one thing to be in the Sacrament, and dissent in the manner of being there. I, being fully by God's Word thereunto persuaded, confess Christ's natural body to be in the Sacrament, indeed, by *spirit and grace*; because that whosoever receiveth worthily that bread and wine, receiveth effectually Christ's body and drinketh His blood; that is, he is made effectually a partaker of His passion; and you make *a grosser* kind of being, enclosing a natural, a lively, and a moving body, under the shape or form of bread and wine.

"Now, this difference considered, to the question thus I answer; that in the Sacrament of the Altar is the natural body and blood of Christ, *verè-realiter, indeed, and really*, if you take these terms *indeed and really*, for spiritually by grace and efficacy; for so every worthy receiver receiveth the very true body of Christ; but if you mean *really and indeed*, so that thereby you would include a lively and a movable body under the forms of bread and wine, then in that sense is not Christ's body in the Sacrament *really and indeed.*"

Such are the words of Bishop Ridley, only a few days before

his martyrdom! I next turned to the Twenty-eighth Article of our religion, and found, "The body of Christ is given, taken, and eaten, in the supper, *only* after an heavenly and spiritual manner. And the mean whereby the body of Christ is received and eaten in the Supper is faith."

Now, reconciling oneself to this truth, there is no difficulty in understanding that part of the sixth chapter of St. John, "Except ye eat the flesh of the Son of Man and drink His blood, ye have no life in you."

The Jews asked the question, "How can this Man give us His flesh to eat?" Nicodemus asked a similar one with respect to the Sacrament of Baptism; both were in unbelief; and I would put it to those Clergymen who have put themselves so prominently forward to condemn the Church of Rome for *her heresy*, and those of the Church of England who are certainly going beyond the line of prudence, if it is not *just possible* they themselves are guilty of the same offence? For what is the meaning of the term "Heresy?" Walker gives it as follows :—" *An opinion of private men different from that of the Catholic and Orthodox Church;*" and he gives the meaning of the word "Heretic :" " *One who propagates his private opinions in opposition to the Catholic Church.*"

I fear I am trespassing too much on your space for one week; but will, with your permission, resume it next, and shall bring that ingredient "*Consistency*" to bear, wherever I find it wanting, in Church matters.

I beg to subscribe myself yours faithfully,

A CHURCHWARDEN.

NORTH WILTS, *Dec.* 18, 1866.

LETTER II.

To the Editor of the "Devizes Gazette."

DEAR SIR,—I concluded my last letter by quoting Walker's definition of the words Heresy and Heretic; and as *truth is truth* all the world over, let us see whether there is any heresy to be found beyond the pale of the Romish Church! We will take the Sacrament of Baptism; and here it is to be lamented that, at Oxford and Cambridge, the schools for *teaching those* who are to teach and instruct their parishioners in after-life, truth and error are both to be learnt there; or, at all events, if error is not taught there, it is imbibed; and we find clergymen educated there, located in two adjoining parishes, the one teaching regeneration in baptism, the other *denying it*, and saying that regeneration or the new birth takes place in after-life, when a man becomes *converted*. Now it is impossible *that both these opinions can be right*; and what a serious matter it becomes, that any member of the Church should hold an erroneous opinion! I verily thought, in my early days with the low Church (as it is called), that regeneration did not take place in baptism; but when I found out my mistake with respect to the other Sacrament, I thought I would look more closely into this; moreover, I had a family of young children, christening nearly one a year; and it was a serious thing (*for which I was responsible*) to teach them otherwise than the truth; and, again, if my child was to receive the benefit of the Sacrament through the FAITH OF its parents, how I hazarded his welfare through my ignorance! I first looked deeply to the teaching of the Church. I looked to see who compiled our Prayer Book, and found the names of *Dr. Cranmer*, Archbishop of Canterbury; Dr. Goodrich, Bishop of Ely; Dr. Skipp, Bishop of Hereford; Dr. Thirlby, Bishop of Westminster; Dr. Day, Bishop of Chichester; Dr. Holbeck, Bishop of Lincoln; *Dr. Ridley*, Bishop of Rochester; Dr. May, Dean of St. Paul's; Dr. Taylor, Dean of Lincoln; Dr. Heynes, Dean of Exeter; Dr. Redman, Dean of Westminster; Dr. Cox, King Edward's Almoner; Dr. M. Robinson, Archdeacon of Leicester.

I thought, if the names of Cranmer and Ridley were there, surely they knew as much as I did, or somewhat more; so I looked to the *service* which they had compiled for the Sacrament, and found that, in the former part, prayers were made to the Almighty, that He would give His "Holy Spirit to *this infant*, that *he*, being BORN AGAIN, and being made *an heir* of everlasting salvation," &c.; that "by the Baptism of Thy well-beloved Son Jesus Christ in the river Jordan, didst *sanctify water to the mystical* WASHING AWAY OF SIN," &c. "We call upon Thee for this infant that *he*, coming to Thy holy baptism, *may receive remission of his sins* by spiritual regeneration," &c.—"Sanctify this water *to the mystical washing away of sin.*" These prayers I found in the service preceding the child's being baptized; and, afterwards, the congregation are addressed as follows: "Seeing now, dearly beloved brethren, that *this child* IS REGENERATE, and grafted into the body of Christ's Church," &c., and then again, "We yield Thee hearty thanks, most merciful Father, that it hath pleased Thee *to regenerate this infant* with Thy Holy Spirit, to receive him for Thine own *child* by adoption, and to incorporate him into Thy holy Church." All this had never struck me before, but I no longer doubted its truth; still I thought I would look further. There was "*the Catechism*," by which the Church taught her children. I found the question, "What is the inward and spiritual grace," in the Sacrament of Baptism? Answer, "*A death unto sin*, and a *new birth* unto righteousness; for, being by *nature born in sin*, and the children of wrath, we are *hereby made* the children of grace."

As the Bereans of old were more noble than the Thessalonians, because they looked to see "if these things were so," so I determined to see if Scripture supported the view the Church had evidently taken. As she had alluded in the Service to our Saviour's Baptism in the river Jordan, as "*sanctifying water*," I turned to that, and found the Baptist telling Him there was no need for Him to be baptized; (that was) *He had no sin to be cleansed of;*

but that, as it was necessary He should be baptized " to fulfil all righteousness," he did it ; and as there is *no other instance* given of the *reality* of the Sacrament, let all, but more especially those clergymen who deny regeneration, consider well the result ! When the Baptist used " the outward and visible sign," WATER, *the Heavens opened*, and the Spirit of God descended upon the Saviour, and a voice from Heaven said, " This is my Son (*in baptism*), in whom I am well pleased." And where is the cold unbeliever who will assert that in *every case* where infants are brought *by faith*, and made sons in baptism, cleansed of the old Adam—viz. "*original sin*," that the Almighty does not give His Spirit, and welcome him as His beloved son (in baptism) in whom He is well pleased?

Let it not be supposed that I would presume to place here any of mankind on an equal footing with the Saviour ; still, as we are made " *sons of God* " in baptism, and the Church teaches the child as soon as it can lisp, to say " OUR FATHER, which art in Heaven," I am not afraid that I have overdrawn the reality, which it is pleasing to think of.

But I thought I would look still further, and take the case of an adult ; so I turned to St. Paul, and found that it was termed " The *Conversion* of St. Paul," when it was made known to him in his journey to Damascus " that he was kicking against the pricks." Well, said I, this is the stumbling-block of the Low Church ; let us see when his *regeneration* took place. I read on, but could find nothing to satisfy me in that account ; but in the twenty-second chapter of the Acts of the Apostles, I found *him* giving a description of his baptism, in his defence to the chief captain and the people. " And one Ananias, a devout man according to the law, having a good report of all the Jews which dwelt there, came unto me, and stood, and said unto me, Brother Saul, receive thy sight. And the same hour I looked up upon him. And he said, The God of our fathers hath chosen thee, that thou shouldest know His will, and see that Just One, and shouldest hear the voice of His mouth. For thou shalt be His witness unto all men of what thou hast seen and heard. And now why tarriest thou ? arise, and be baptized, *and wash away thy sins*, calling on the name of the Lord."

Can it be necessary to produce any further evidence ? Still, here it is, in the second chapter of the Acts, when Peter, the mouthpiece of the other eleven Apostles, told the Jews on the day of Pentecost, when they asked, " Men and Brethren, what shall we do ? Then Peter said unto them, Repent and be baptized *every one of you* in the name of Jesus Christ, *for the remission of sins*, and ye shall *receive the gift of the Holy Ghost*."

Surely the Church, if she is orthodox, can teach *nothing less* than regeneration. And every time we repeat the *Nicene Creed*, " I acknowledge *one Baptism for the remission of sins*," what description of religion is ours if we *don't believe it?*

Let us next look to the CONSISTENCY of those ministers of the Church of England who are so loud in the condemnation of others. Whether they have ever looked on their own holy office seriously, and can justify their position, I know not ; but this I know, that the Church of Rome—though *she has no right to be called so in this country* (as where can we read of St. Paul, writing *to the Church of Rome*, which was at Corinth, or Ephesus, or Galatia, or Thessalonica, or Colosse? Or, suppose that he had written to *the Church* which was *in England*, if she was Christianized at that time, would he also have included *the Church of Rome* WHICH IS IN ENGLAND ?)—even the Roman Catholics are consistent, so far as thinking all the world is subject to her, and trying to maintain their claim ! The Dissenters too, who cannot believe in the doctrine of the Church, and keep without her pale, are consistent also ; and even those men (so much abused) who, through their *impatience*, have left our Church for that of Rome, act a consistent part in comparison of those who *dissent* from her doctrines, whether *High* or *Low*, and still remain, administering her Sacraments and teaching her children what " *The Church* " has never sanctioned. What can we say of those clergymen who, baptizing an infant, supplicate the Almighty, to " *sanctify* that water *to the mystical washing away of sins, and pray*, that that child might be born again." And afterwards THANK Almighty God that he is become *regenerate*, and declare the same to the congregation ! What, I say, can be said of such, who having gone through the service, *do not believe it ;* where is the CONSISTENCY of these men *remaining in our Church?* I can respect the honest Dissenter ; but the holy office alone that they hold demands my esteem !

I may be told that *they* put a different construction on those parts of the Service I have mentioned ; but *that* is a rather dangerous practice, as St. Peter and St. Paul say, " The Scriptures are not of *private interpretation ;*" and if every one is to twist them about to suit *his own purpose*, will not the Church of Rome have good cause to maintain that *the Bible* should not be given to the laity? They might say, better to be in ignorance and obedient, than to misconstrue the truth, and cause the divisions, or otherwise, the heresies and schisms we unfortunately find in our Church. But I am again trespassing too long on your space, and will crave further room next week, when I hope to show that our Church stands prominently forward as the English branch of the Church Catholic !

I remain, Sir, yours faithfully,

A CHURCHWARDEN.

NORTH WILTS, *Dec. 22nd*, 1866.

see what constitutes a Church. If we go back to the days of Adam we shall find the Church consisted of him and his wife ; we shall see the holy estate of matrimony instituted, and the Scripture declaring, "Therefore shall a man leave his father and his mother, and shall cleave unto his wife, and they *twain* shall be *one flesh*." After our first parents were joined together by the Almighty Himself, it was necessary there should be a Church on earth to perform such *a mystery*. And we find the Patriarchs styled, "Priests and Kings" in their families.

It is interesting to trace the Church of God through the Old Testament : we find it existing in the person of Abel ; then again, Eve rejoicing at the birth of Seth. She makes no mention of her other children ; but here she seems to foresee the future : "For God," *said she*, "hath appointed me another seed *instead of Abel*, whom Cain slew." "And to Seth was born Enos. Then began men to call upon the name of the Lord." Next is given the genealogy of ten generations from Adam to Noah, including Enoch and Methusaleh, when we come to this remarkable passage —"And it came to pass when men began to multiply on the face of the earth, and daughters were born unto them, that the *sons of God* saw the daughters of men that they were fair, and they took them wives of all which they chose."

Here was the *visible Church* mingling with idolatry ; and the result was such an amount of wickedness as to cause the Almighty to destroy the world by a flood. This brings us over a space of 1656 years ; and then we find the Church on Mount Ararat, consisting of only eight souls. "And Noah builded an altar unto the Lord, and took of every clean beast, and of every clean fowl, and offered burnt offerings on the altar. And the Lord smelled a sweet savour ; and the Lord said in His heart, I will not again curse the ground any more for man's sake."

We next come to the eleventh chapter of Genesis, and find the "Church visible" through the family of Shem, the son of Noah, and ten more generations to Abram, called Abraham, when God made a covenant with him, "*The covenant of Circumcision*." It had now existed 2106 years. We find, too, that mysterious person, Melchizedek, king of Salem, "the Priest of the Most High God," blessing Abram, and receiving "Tythe" of him ! Then we see it in the line of Jacob, Isaac's *youngest* son ; and we see, in the thirty-fifth chapter, the Almighty blessing Jacob, and changing his name to Israel.

We follow Israel into Egypt, and find them in bondage, and Moses and Aaron raised up for their deliverance ; and, finally, leaving Egypt, and going into the wilderness of Sin. And after three months, when the Church had existed 2513 years, we find them in the wilderness of Sinai, at the foot of the mountain. Here the Almighty delivered the law of the ten commandments to Moses, to give to the children of Israel ; here, too, we see more fully what is *required* by the Almighty of those who form His Church :—"And the Lord spake unto Moses, saying, Speak unto the children of Israel that they *bring Me an offering*: of every man that giveth it willingly with his heart, ye shall take My offering ; and this is the offering which ye shall take of them : *gold, and silver, and brass, and blue, and purple, and scarlet, &c.!* And let them make Me a SANCTUARY, that I may dwell among them."

Instructions are given for the altar, the ark, and for the service, and Aaron and his sons *set apart* for the *Priest's office,* the ceremonies of consecrating the Priests ; and, in the eighth chapter of Leviticus, we find Moses commanded to consecrate Aaron and his sons, and the manner in which he did it ! We see next, " Nadab and Abihu," *two of the sons of Aaron,* destroyed by fire, for offering *strange fire* to the Almighty ; we find, too, the tribe of Levi set apart for the service and ministry of the sanctuary ; being the first instance of a *threefold* ministry in God's Church, and which, I believe, *has existed from that time to the present!* Aaron was the High Priest, his sons were under him as Priests, and the Levites were under both, ministering in the Tabernacle.

We come now to an era in the Church in the wilderness, which Christians of all denominations in the present day will do well to study—" THE REBELLION OF KORAH," in the sixteenth chapter of Numbers :—" Now Korah the son of Izhar, the son of Kohath, *the son of Levi,* and Dathan and Abiram, the sons of Eliab, and On, the son of Peleth, *sons of Reuben,* took men. And they rose up before Moses, with certain of the children of Israel," &c. &c. They rebelled against Moses, and offered strange fire unto the Lord. " And Moses said unto Korah, Hear, I pray you, ye sons of Levi ; seemeth it but a small thing unto you, that the God of Israel hath separated you from the congregation of Israel, to bring you near to Himself, to do the service of the Tabernacle of the Lord, and to stand before the congregation, to minister unto them ? And He hath brought thee near *to Him,* and all thy brethren the sons of Levi with thee : *and seek ye the Priesthood also?"*

This was their sin, and their punishment was as follows :— " And it came to pass, as Moses had made an end of speaking all these words, that the ground clave asunder that was under them ; and the earth opened her mouth, and swallowed them up, and their houses, and all the men that *appertained* unto Korah, and all their goods.—They, and all that *appertained* unto them, went down alive into the pit, and the earth closed upon them : and they *perished from among the congregation."*

" The Lord also said *to* Moses, Speak to Eleazar the Priest, that he take the censers of these sinners against their own souls, and make broad plates for the altar ; for they were hallowed," being offered before the Lord. " To be *a sign* unto the children of Israel, that NO STRANGER which is not of the seed of Aaron, come near to offer incense before the Lord."

The eighteenth chapter of Numbers gives a clear description of the Priest's and Levite's office, and *their portion.* " And, behold, I have given the children of Levi all the TENTH in Israel, for an inheritance, for their service which they serve, even the service of the Tabernacle of the congregation."—The next significant point is the death of Aaron the High Priest: "And the Lord spake unto Moses, saying, Take Aaron and Eleazar his son, and bring them up unto Mount Hor: and strip Aaron of his garments, *and put them upon Eleazar his son:* and Aaron shall be gathered unto his people, and shall die there. And Moses did as the Lord commanded." The death of Moses is the next to notice, and the appointment of Joshua in his stead. "And the Lord said unto Moses, Take thee Joshua, the son of Nun, a man in whom is the spirit, and *lay thine hand upon him,* and set him before *Eleazar the Priest,* and before all the congregation; and give him a charge in their sight. And thou shalt put some of thine honour upon him, that all the congregation of the children of Israel *may be obedient.*"

The Church, with the Ark of God, now approaches the promised land of Canaan, and as Moses was not (like Aaron) to enter it, he ascended Mount Nebo, and the Lord showed him all the land of Canaan, and he died there on the Mount.—Joshua then takes the command; and, as he approaches the river Jordan, it, like the Red Sea, divided to let them pass through. We then see him driving out all the nations before him, and find him at the end of the Book of Joshua, settling the tribes of Israel in their inheritance, and then died; Eleazar the High Priest died also. The Church had now existed 2584 years!—Fourteen years afterwards, we find Phineas, the son of Eleazar, as High Priest; and in the sixth chapter of the first of Chronicles, we find the line of the Priests, and also of Aaron and his sons, *who succeeded him* as High Priests:—"But Aaron and his sons offered upon the altar of the burnt-offering, and on the altar of incense, *and were appointed* for all the work of the place most holy, and to make an atonement for Israel; and these are the sons of Aaron: Eleazar his son, Phineas his son, Abishua his son, Bukki his son, Uzzi his son, Zerahia his son, Meraioth his son, Amariah his son, Ahitub his son, Zadok his son, Ahimaaz his son."

We next find, in the Book of Samuel, Saul is anointed the first King over Israel; and is succeeded by David, and Solomon his son, who builds the magnificent Temple at Jerusalem; and, in the sixth chapter of the Second of Chronicles, we find his beautiful prayer at the dedication of it, and which is *the first lesson in the Service of Consecration of all our Churches!*

Rehoboam, the son of Solomon, succeeds him. Ten tribes revolt to Jeroboam, and henceforth the Tribes of Israel are described as Israel, and Judah, and the King of Israel as "Jeroboam the son of Nebat, who made Israel to sin." They sinned on through nineteen generations of kings; till, in the reign of Hoshea, Shalmaneser, the King of Assyria, went up and besieged Samaria.—"In the ninth year of Hoshea, the King of Assyria took Samaria, and carried Israel away captive into Assyria, and placed them in Halah and in Habor, by the river Gozan, and in the cities of the Medes." "And the Lord removed Israel out of His sight, as He had said by all His servants the prophets. So was Israel carried away out of their own land to Assyria, unto this day." The Church is henceforth to be seen in the Tribe of Judah. " Therefore the Lord was very angry with Israel, *and removed them out of His sight:* there was none left but the Tribe of Judah only."— The Tribe of Benjamin formed a part of Judah, with the Priests and Levites, and these constitute the Church, who in the reign of Zedekiah became so sinful, that God's mercy and patience were worn out : "And the wrath of the Lord arose against His people, till there was no remedy." He brought upon them the King of the Chaldees, who had no compassion on them, but slew a great number, and burnt Jerusalem and the Temple with fire, and took all that remained captive to Babylon. Here they remained in captivity till the first year of the reign of Cyrus the Persian.

We read in the Book of Ezra, " Thus saith Cyrus King of Persia, the Lord God of heaven hath given me all the kingdoms of the earth, and He hath charged me to build Him an house at Jerusalem, which is in Judah. Who is there among you of all His people ? His God be with him, and let him go up to Jerusalem, which is in Judah, and build the house of the Lord God of Israel (He is the God) which is in Jerusalem.

" Then rose up the chief of the fathers of Judah and Benjamin, and the Priests and the Levites, with all them whose spirit God had raised to go up, to build the house of the Lord which is in Jerusalem." In the second chapter we see the number that returned ; and in the sixty-first and sixty-second verses, thus :— "And the children of the Priests, the children of Habaiah, the children of Koz, the children of Barzillai. These sought their register *among* those that were reckoned *by genealogy,* but they were not found, therefore were they, as polluted, *put from the Priesthood."*

I have often heard people speak of the *ten* " *lost tribes of Israel,"* that looking through the nations of the world they can nowhere be recognized ; but if the prophetic language of Ezekiel, in his vision of dry bones has been fulfilled, a remnant of them, or a tenth, as is elsewhere said, should return to Judah. The thirty-seventh chapter fully explains this, and at verse 21, " And thou shalt say unto them, Thus saith the Lord God, Behold, I will take the children of Israel *from among the heathen* whither they be gone, and will gather them on every side, and bring them into their own land. And I will make them *one nation* in the land upon the mountains of Israel, and *one king* shall be king to them all ; and they shall be no more two nations, neither shall they be divided into *two kingdoms* any more at all. And David my servant shall be king over them ; and they all shall have one shepherd ; they shall also walk in my judgments, and observe my statutes, and do them." As David had been dead more than 400 years when this prophecy was written, it was his successors on the throne *of Judah* that were to reign over them.

The Bible tells us but very little more respecting the whereabouts of the Jews ; we find Jehoiachin, King of Judah, in the

B

thirty-seventh year of their captivity, taken from prison by the King of Babylon, and his throne set above the kings that were with him in Babylon, and we find the whole of them going to Jerusalem after the second Temple was built! This was 457 years before Christ, and, consequently, the Church had existed 3547 years.

Tradition, I have no doubt, will fill up the space of these four centuries and a half. The first chapter of Matthew only tells us that there were fourteen generations from the captivity to the birth of Christ, and that Herod was King of Judea at that time, and that the Priests and Levites still existed in the Church.

We may gather, then, from this brief history, that as soon as the Almighty had a sanctuary, or tabernacle, built Him, " That HE might *dwell* among His people," He ordained three orders of the ministry—the High Priest, the Priests, the sons of Aaron, and their successors—and the Tribe of Levi wholly set apart for the service of the sanctuary! In the case of Nadab and Abihu, and Korah, Dathan, and Abiram, the awful punishment they received for daring to offer strange fire, and a warning given to the Jews, that NO STRANGER should presume to take upon him the Priest's office! We again find when the Jews returned from captivity, and the Priests were required *to prove their genealogy,* that three families could not do it, and they were *put from the Priesthood,* AS POLLUTED!

Such is the history of the Church of God during the lives of the Patriarchs to the time of our Saviour; and as my letter is already too long, I must leave till next week the transition state of the Jewish and the Christian Church! And remain

Yours truly,
A CHURCHWARDEN.

NORTH WILTS, *Jan.* 7, 1867.

LETTER IV.

To the Editor of the " Devizes Gazette."

DEAR SIR,—In my last letter I traced the Patriarchal and the Jewish Church up to the time of our Saviour: it existed without change for twenty-nine years, during His infancy, and on to His manhood, till He took upon Himself the office of High Priest. We find Him conforming to its rules, " circumcised the eighth day," and when He was twelve years old, going up to Jerusalem with His parents to keep the feast of the Passover. And as *His custom was,* He went into the Synagogue on the Sabbath day." And when He began to preach, in His beautiful sermon on the mount, He said, " Think not that I am come to destroy the law or the prophets : I am not come to destroy, but to fulfil. For verily I say unto you, till heaven and earth pass, *one jot, or one tittle,* shall in no wise pass from the law, till all be fulfilled."

The preaching and ministry of our Saviour, I will term the transition state between the Jewish and the Christian Church ; and the first person we have to notice is John the Baptist. " Behold I send My messenger before Thy face, which shall prepare Thy way before Thee."—" John did baptize in the wilderness, and preach the baptism of repentance *for the remission of sins.*" And we find our Saviour in the sixteenth chapter of St. Luke, saying " The law and the prophets were until John : *since that time* the kingdom of God is preached." Still we can only look on the Church as in a transition state, as the Jewish ceremonies and worship were kept up, our Saviour fulfilling his part, as when He healed the leper, He said unto him, " See thou tell no man, but go thy way, shew thyself *to the Priest,* and offer the gift *that Moses commanded.*" And again, when the ten lepers were healed—" Go, shew yourselves unto the Priests, and it came to pass that as they went they were cleansed."

John the Baptist was the son of Zacharias the HIGH PRIEST, and he (*no stranger*) was sent to prepare the way for the High Priest of the Christian Church ! We find, then, at the birth of Christ *the three-fold ministry* existing as before—the High Priest, the Priests, and Levites—and when our Saviour began His ministry, He may well be termed the High Priest ; and then we find Him calling *and ordaining* His twelve Apostles. " And when He had called His twelve disciples He gave them power against unclean spirits, to cast them out, and to heal all manner of sickness, and all manner of disease ;" and sent them forth, saying, " Go not into the way of the Gentiles, but go rather to the lost sheep of the house of Israel. And as ye go, preach, saying, The kingdom of heaven is at hand." " *And whosoever shall not receive you, nor hear your words,* when you depart out of that house, or city, shake off the dust of your feet ; verily I say unto you, it shall be more tolerable for the land of Sodom and Gomorrah in the day of judgment than for that city."

We read, too, in the tenth chapter of St. Luke—" After these things the Lord appointed *other seventy also,* and sent them two and two before His face into every city and place whither He Himself would come."

These seem (like the Levites in the Jewish Church) to have *less authority* given them than the twelve Apostles ; still there is the same sentence of condemnation against *all those* who would not receive them, as in the former case.

Here, then, we find again, a *three-fold ministry* in this transition state of the Church—Jesus, the High Priest ; the twelve Apostles ; and the seventy Disciples !

It is not necessary for my purpose to quote much of our Saviour's ministry, but we will note (*as it has been questioned by a Wiltshire Incumbent*) the third chapter of St. John, twenty-second verse—" After these things came Jesus and His disciples into the land of Judea, and there He tarried with them, *and baptized.*" But it is said in the next chapter—" Though Jesus Himself baptized not, but His disciples." As a matter of course, *with His au-*

thority, and shewing that the act of baptizing was left to the inferior clergy, the same as when Peter was in the house of Cornelius the Gentiles receiving the Holy Ghost, "He *commanded* them to be baptized in the name of the Lord."

I mentioned at the beginning of my last letter, the institution of the Holy estate of Matrimony ! Our Saviour now treats of it Himself in the nineteenth chapter of Matthew—"The Pharisees also came unto Him, tempting Him, and saying unto Him, Is it lawful for a man to put away his wife for every cause ? And He said unto them, Have ye not read, that He which made them at the beginning made them male and female ? and said, for this cause shall a man leave father and mother, and shall cleave to his wife : and they twain shall be one flesh. Wherefore they are *no more twain, but one flesh.* What, therefore, GOD *hath joined together* let not man put asunder."

I shall have occasion again to refer to this, as there is a long difference between this description of matrimony, and that performed at the "BOARD OF GUARDIANS ! "

The time is now come, when our Saviour, having planted His Church by choosing His twelve Apostles and the seventy Disciples, is about to make the great sacrifice promised to Adam, and prefigured through the whole of the Old Testament ; but before He leaves the world, He makes that beautifully solemn prayer that we find in the seventeenth chapter of St. John, where He prays His heavenly Father to glorify Him, and to preserve His Apostles in *unity* and *truth !*—" I have manifested Thy name unto the men which Thou gavest Me out of the world : Thine they were, and thou gavest them Me ; and they have kept Thy word. And now I am no more in the world, but *these* are in the world, and I come to Thee. Holy Father, keep through Thine own name those whom Thou hast given Me, that *they may be one, as we are.* I pray not that Thou shouldest take them out of the world, but that Thou shouldest keep them from the evil. Neither pray I for these alone, but for them also which shall believe on Me *through their word ;* that they all *may be one,* as Thou, Father, art in Me, and I in Thee ; that they also *may be one in us* ; THAT THE WORLD MAY BELIEVE THAT THOU HAST SENT ME."

The Saviour now makes the great atonement for sin, and for a time the Christian Church has but two orders in the ministry—the eleven Apostles, and the seventy Disciples—but we may look upon it as in a state of abeyance, as we find in the first chapter of the Acts of the Apostles they were bid not to depart from Jerusalem ; " but *wait* for the promise of the Father, which, saith He, ye have heard of Me."

The Jewish Church has been one of authority up to this time ; and we find the High Priest, the Chief Priests, and the multitude of the Jews demanding the Saviour's death ; and when Pilate washed his hands and said, " I am innocent of the blood of this just person, see ye to it." " Then answered all the people and said, HIS BLOOD BE ON US AND ON OUR CHILDREN." And sure enough it has been, for although they still exist as a people they have no nation, and are scattered over the face of the whole earth.

As *the Christian Church* is now established, let us see what authority is given to those that our Saviour left behind Him at His death? He had made the great atonement, but He had evidently left *a portion of His work unfinished;* and St. Luke tells us, in the first chapter of the Acts of the Apostles, "The former treatise have I made, O Theophilus, of all that Jesus began both to do and teach, until the day in which He was taken up, *after that He, through the Holy Ghost, had given commandments unto the Apostles whom He had chosen.* To whom also He showed Himself alive after His passion, by many infallible proofs, being seen of them forty days, *and speaking of the things pertaining to the kingdom of God."*

St. Matthew tells us Jesus came to the eleven Disciples and said unto them, "All power is given unto Me in heaven and in earth. Go *ye* therefore and teach all nations, baptizing them in the name of the Father, and of the Son, and of the Holy Ghost; teaching them to observe all things whatsoever I have commanded you: and lo, *I am with you alway, even unto the end of the world."*

St. Mark says, "Afterward He appeared unto the eleven, as they sat at meat, and upbraided them with their unbelief and hardness of heart, because they believed not them which had seen Him after He was risen. And He said unto them, Go *ye* into all the world, and preach the Gospel to every creature. He that believeth and is baptized shall be saved; *but he that believeth not shall be damned."*

St. Luke tells us, "Then opened He their understanding, *that they might understand the Scriptures."* And in the twentieth chapter of St. John we read: "Then said Jesus unto them again, Peace be unto you: as my Father hath sent Me, *even so send I you.* And when He had said this, *He breathed on them,* and saith unto them, *Receive ye the Holy Ghost. Whosoever sins ye remit, they are remitted unto them; and whosoever sins ye retain, they are retained."*

Having given the Apostles authority as above, and promised them that they should be baptized with the Holy Ghost not many days hence, we read in the first chapter of Acts, "When they therefore were come together, they asked of Him saying, Lord, wilt Thou at *this time restore again* the kingdom to Israel? And He said unto them, It is not for you to know the times or the seasons which the Father hath put in His own power. But ye shall receive power after that the Holy Ghost is come upon you: and ye shall be witnesses unto Me, both in Jerusalem and in all Judea, and in Samaria, *and unto the uttermost part of the earth.* And when He had spoken these things, while they beheld, He was taken up; and a cloud received Him out of their sight."

There is no doubt whatever respecting the true commission and authority given by the Saviour *to the eleven Apostles,* after that He arose from the dead; and we find the first thing they did was to fill up the vacancy caused by the death of the traitor Judas "In

those days Peter stood up in the midst of the Disciples, and said,
—Men and brethren, this scripture must needs have been fulfilled,
which the Holy Ghost by the mouth of David spake before concerning Judas, which was guide to them that took Jesus, for he
was numbered with us, and had obtained part of this ministry, &c.
—For it is written in the Book of Psalms, Let his habitation be
desolate, and let no man dwell therein ; and *his bishopric* let another take.—Wherefore *of these men* (the seventy Disciples) which
have companied with us all the time that the Lord Jesus went in
and out among us, beginning from the baptism of John until that
same day that He was taken up from us, *must one be ordained* to
be a witness with us of His resurrection. And they appointed
two, Joseph called Barsabas, and Matthias. And they gave forth
their lots, and the lot fell upon Matthias, *and he was numbered
with the eleven Apostles.*"

The Jews were the peculiar people of the Almighty : they are
now invited to believe in the Saviour and join the Christian
Church ! The twelve Apostles, the seventy Disciples, John the
Baptist, in fact all who have taken any part hitherto in the Church
were Jews, and we find St. Peter when he went to Cornelius, the
Centurion, saying, unto him, " Ye know how, that it is an *unlaw-
ful thing* for a man that is a Jew, to keep company with, or come
unto one of another nation ; but God hath showed me that I should
not call any man common or unclean." Here was the calling of
the Gentiles, and all the world into *the Christian Church,* as our
Saviour said, " And *other sheep* I have, which are not of this fold ;
them also I must bring, and they shall hear My voice ; and there
shall be one fold and one Shepherd."

We find in the second chapter of Acts by the preaching of
Peter three thousand souls were added to the Church, and that
" The Lord added to the Church daily *such as should be saved.*" In
the fourth chapter again, that five thousand believed ; and at the
thirty-second verse, " And the multitude of them that believed,
were of one heart, and of one soul ! "

The *third order of the Priesthood in the Christian Church* is now
to be appointed, and we read in the sixth chapter of the Acts,
" Then *the twelve* called the multitude of the disciples unto them,
and said, It is not reason that we should leave the Word of God,
and serve tables. Wherefore, *brethren,* look ye out *among you*
seven men of honest report, full of the Holy Ghost and wisdom,
whom *we may appoint* over this business. And the saying pleased
the whole multitude, and they chose Stephen, and Philip, and
Prochorus, and Nicanor, and Timon, and Parmenas, and Nicholas,
whom they set *before the Apostles;* and when they had prayed,
they laid their hands upon them. And the Word of the Lord increased ; and the number of the disciples multiplied in Jerusalem
greatly ; *and a great company* OF THE PRIESTS were obedient to the
faith." In the eighth chapter we see the Church planted in
Samaria, by Philip ; and in the ninth chapter the " miraculous
conversion of St. Paul." In the twelfth chapter we find, " But
the word of God grew and multiplied. And Barnabas and Saul

returned from Jerusalem, when they had fulfilled their ministry, and took with them John, whose surname was Mark." The next chapter begins thus ; "Now there were in *the Church* that was at Antioch, certain prophets and teachers ; as Barnabas, and Simeon, and Lucius, and Manaen, and Saul. As they ministered to the Lord, and fasted, the Holy Ghost said, Separate me *Barnabas and Saul, for the work whereunto I have called them.* And when they fasted and prayed, *and laid their hands on them,* they sent them away. So they being sent forth by the Holy Ghost, departed unto Seleucia ; and from thence they sailed to Cyprus."

I must here make a digression, to introduce *a similar instance* in the English Church at the present time !!! Separate me Milman and Butler, *for the work whereunto I have called them!!!* And *when the hands* OF OUR BISHOPS *have been laid upon them,* they will be sent away to the work appointed for them to do !!!

The three orders of the ministry in the Christian Church, which our Saviour and His Apostles had established, consisted of the twelve Apostles, or Elders, or *Bishops*; the seventy and other Disciples, or Presbyters, or *Priests;* and the *seven Deacons*. And when we say, every time we repeat the Nicene Creed, "*I believe in one Catholick and Apostolic Church*," it is *every national* branch of THIS CHURCH, which makes it Catholic, or universal ; and it was founded by the Apostles which makes it Apostolick ! I am again encroaching too much on your space, so remain,

Yours truly,
A CHURCHWARDEN.

NORTH WILTS, *Jan.* 21, 1867.

LETTER V.

To the Editor of the "Devizes Gazette."

DEAR SIR,—In my last letter I traced the Christian Church to the appointment of the seven Deacons, completing therein *the three orders of the ministry,* the same as had existed in the Jewish Church, and in that in which our Saviour ministered. The Disciples it seems were first called Christians in Antioch, and now I shall follow the Acts of the Apostles to see how far our English Church conforms to the doctrine laid down by them.

We find Paul and Barnabas going to Lystra and Derbe, CITIES of Lycaonia, and to Iconium, and Antioch, confirming the souls of the Disciples :—"And when they had ordained them *elders in every Church,* and had prayed with fasting, they commended them to the Lord, on whom they believed." We find Timothy ordained the *first Bishop* of the Church of the Ephesians, and Titus the *first Bishop* of the Cretians, and St. Paul writing to Titus—"For this cause left I thee in Crete, that thou shouldest *set in order* the things that are wanting, and *ordain elders in every city,* as I had appointed thee." That these elders were Bishops, is proved by

the next two verses—" If any be blameless, the husband of one
wife," &c. " For a BISHOP must be blameless, as the steward of
God," &c. And St. Peter writes in his first epistle—" The elders
which are among you, I exhort, *who am also an elder.*"
    Our English Church is here completely Apostolic ; for we have
no CITY without a Bishop, and we have no Bishopric without a
CITY. When Dr. Lee was ordained Bishop of Manchester,
which was only a *borough town,* Manchester was made a *city* to
receive a Bishop ! It is true, that through the niggardliness of the
State, in some few instances, we have *two cities* with only ONE
BISHOP, such as " London and Westminster," " Bath and Wells,"
" Gloucester and Bristol ;" but as a rule we have, as I before
stated, no city without an elder or Bishop. I must here mention,
too, another instance of the State's great care and affection for the
Church : that when Dr. Lee was created Bishop of Manchester,
our Liberal Government, fearing the Church would be too strongly
represented in the House of Peers, and be able to defend herself
against her numerous enemies, decided that the junior Bishop in
the Church should be *without a seat* in that august assembly.
    The fifteenth chapter of the Acts begins—" And certain men
which came down from Judea, taught the brethren, and said,
" Except ye be circumcised after the manner of Moses, ye cannot
be saved. When therefore Paul and Barnabas had no small dissension with them, they determined that Paul and Barnabas, and
certain others with them, should go up *to Jerusalem unto the
Apostles and elders* about this question." " And when they were
come to Jerusalem, they were received of the Church, and of the
Apostles and elders." " And the Apostles and elders came
together for to consider of this matter." Peter, and Barnabas,
and Paul seem to have argued the point. " And after they had
held their peace, JAMES (the metropolitan Bishop of Jerusalem)
answered, saying, Men and brethren, hearken unto me," &c.
" Wherefore *my sentence is,* that we trouble not them which from
among the Gentiles are turned to God," &c.
    This is the first council held in the Christian Church, and the
result was as follows :—" Then pleased it the Apostles and elders,
with the whole Church, to send chosen men of their own company
to Antioch ; and wrote letters by them after this manner, The
Apostles and elders and brethren send greeting unto the brethren
which are of the Gentiles in Antioch, and Syria, and Cilicia. For-
asmuch as we have heard that certain *which went out from us* have
troubled you with words, subverting your souls, saying, ye must
be circumcised, and keep the law ; to whom *we gave no such commandment.*" " It seemed good unto us," &c. The next chapter
tells us that Paul and Silas, when they came to Derbe and Lystra,
" As they went through the cities, they delivered them the decrees
for to keep, that were ordained of the Apostles and elders which
were at Jerusalem. And so were *the Churches established in the
faith,* and increased in number daily."
    We see in the instance above, how any *division* in the early
Christian Church was set at rest, and this appears to have been

the first serious dissension, caused "by certain that went out from the Apostles," *acting without their authority.* The unconverted Jews (who may now be termed a sect) seem to be at this time the only religious opponents of the Christians, "the Pharisees and Sadducees," forming a part of them; and St. Paul, in writing to them in the Epistle to the Hebrews, explains to them the mode of salvation, and urges them to join the Christian faith, and concludes in the last chapter, "Remember them which have the rule over you, who have spoken unto you the word of God: whose faith follow, considering the end of their conversation. Jesus Christ, the same yesterday, and to-day, and for ever. Be not carried about *with divers and strange doctrines;* for it is a good thing that the heart be established with grace, *not with meats,* which have not profited them that have been occupied therein. We have AN ALTAR" (in the Christian Church) "whereof they have no right to eat, which serve the tabernacle," &c. It is here self-evident that the Jews who would not believe from that time to the present, have acted upon their own responsibility, and have shut themselves out from the "new and better covenant," mentioned in the eighth chapter.

And now, would that I could persuade every Dissenter of every denomination to go through this simple history of the Church with me, to follow St. Paul through all his epistles; but before we do this, let us look to the acts and deeds of the Apostles once more! In the twentieth chapter we find—"And from Miletus Paul sent to Ephesus and called *the elders* of the Church," &c., "and he said unto them, Take heed therefore unto yourselves, and to all the flock, over the which the Holy Ghost *hath made you overseers,* to feed the Church of God, which He hath purchased with His own blood. For I know this, that after my departing *shall grievous wolves enter in among you* not sparing the flock. *Also of your* OWN SELVES shall men arise, *speaking perverse things to draw away disciples after them.* Therefore watch, and remember that by the space of three years I ceased not to warn every one night and day WITH TEARS."

Well enough might those tears have been shed, if, when he said, "I KNOW THIS," he could have had any conception of what our English Church is at the present time; but we will follow him through his epistles, and see THE UNITY he conceives necessary for God's Church!!! To the Church which is at Rome he writes, "Now I beseech you, brethren, *mark them which cause divisions and offences, contrary to the doctrine which ye have learned:* and avoid them." To "the Church of God which is at Corinth," we find, "Now I beseech you, brethren, by the name of our Lord Jesus Christ, *that ye all speak the same thing, and that there be no divisions among you;* for it hath been declared unto me, that there are contentions among you. Now this I say, that every one of you saith, I am of Paul, and I of Apollos, and I of Cephas, and I of Christ—Is CHRIST DIVIDED? Was Paul crucified for you?" &c. The Corinthians are here rebuked, not that they left the Church to follow dissent, for Paul, and Apollos, and Cephas, *were all ministers of the Church;* but because they approved of one more than another, the same as if the parishioners of one parish chose to leave their pastor, because they liked the one in the next parish better. How much more serious then the division when we say, I am of the Church, I am of Wesley, and I of Calvin! What would St. Paul say to this, who began his Epistle to the Corinthians as above, and finished as follows :—"Finally, brethren, farewell ; be perfect, be of good comfort, *be of one mind ?*"

In writing to the Galatians, he says, " I marvel, that ye are so soon removed from him that called you into the Grace of Christ, unto another gospel : which is not another ; but there be some that trouble you *and would pervert the gospel of Christ.* As we said before, so say I now again, If any man preach any other gospel unto you, *than that ye have received,* let him be accursed." And again, "O foolish Galatians, who hath bewitched you, that you should not obey the truth."

To the Saints which are at Ephesus, he writes :—" I, therefore, the prisoner of the Lord, beseech you that ye walk worthy of the vocation wherewith ye are called—endeavouring to keep *the unity of the Spirit in the bond of peace.* There is *one body* and *one spirit,* even as ye are called in *one* hope of your calling—*one Lord, one faith, one baptism, one God and Father of all.*" In writing to the Saints at Philippi, with the *Bishops and Deacons,* he says, " If there be therefore any consolation in Christ, if any comfort of love, if any fellowship of the Spirit—fulfil ye my joy, that ye be *like minded,* having the same love, being of *one accord, of one mind.*"

To the Thessalonians, he writes :—" Therefore, brethren, stand fast and hold *the traditions* which ye have been taught, whether by word, or our epistle—and if any man *obey not our word* by this epistle, note that man, and have no company with him, that he may be ashamed." To Timothy, the Bishop of Ephesus, he writes :—" I charge thee, therefore, before God. Preach the word, be instant in season, and out of season ; reprove, rebuke, exhort with all long-suffering and doctrine. For the time will come when they will *not endure sound doctrine;* but after their own lusts shall they heap *to themselves teachers,* having itching ears : *and they shall turn away their ears from the truth,*" &c.

Who can read these quotations from St. Paul's writings, and not lament the " false doctrine, the heresies, and schisms," of the present day.

Again, we find in St. Peter, third chapter—" Finally, *be ye all of one mind :*" and "but there were false prophets also among the people, even as there shall be *false teachers among you,* who privily shall bring in *damnable heresies,*" &c. His last chapter begins thus :—" This second epistle, beloved, I now write unto you ; in both which I stir up your pure minds by way of remembrance ; that ye may be mindful of the words which were spoken before by the holy prophets, *and of the commandment of us the Apostles of the Lord and Saviour.*" St. John, too, writes in his Epistle :—" To try the Spirits, *as many false prophets are gone out into the world.*"

St. Jude finishes this fearful list, complaining that, " there are certain men crept in unawares," &c.—and then, " But, beloved, remember ye the words which were spoken before of the Apostles of our Lord Jesus Christ; how that they told you there should be mockers in the last time, who should walk after their own ungodly lust. *These be they who separate themselves*," &c.

Can there be any doubt of the UNITY that ought to exist in the Church of God—nay, *that must exist?* See what St. John writes to the seven Churches which are in Asia, *national Churches*, of the HOLY JERUSALEM, which he saw in a vision. "And the wall of the city had twelve foundations, and in them the names *of the twelve Apostles of the Lamb.*" "And there shall in no wise enter into it any thing that defileth, neither whatsoever worketh abomination, *or maketh a lie;* but they which are written in the Lamb's book of life."

If the foundation of the New Jerusalem is built on the faith of the Apostles, how careful we should be, in striving to enter in, to walk in their footsteps! And as our Saviour, *in giving them authority* over the Church, promised to be WITH THEM, "*even unto the end of the world*," all those who have received *rightful ordination* according to St. Paul's instructions to Timothy and Titus, are those who, at the present time, *throughout the world*, are the ministers of God's Church. It is the Bible that I have quoted throughout; I have carefully looked to find, if possible, any warrant for dissension. I find St. Paul saying *to the Jews*, " It was necessary that the Word of God should first have been spoken to you ; but seeing ye put it from you, and judge *yourselves unworthy of everlasting life*, lo, we turn to the Gentiles." And in the quotations I have made from his writings, to the Corinthians in particular, it is evident what he thought of divisions and dissent in the early Church. " Demas hath forsaken me, having loved this present world, and *is departed* into Thessalonica." " Hymeneus and Alexander, concerning faith having made shipwreck, I have delivered unto Satan, that they may learn not to blaspheme."

Having been through the whole Bible to show *what constitutes a Church*, I will endeavour in my next to fulfil my intention of illustrating the Church of England apart from the Churches of Rome and Germany, and the evils we are suffering from the introduction of the principles of the latter at the time of the *Glorious Reformation*.

I remain, dear Sir, yours faithfully,

A CHURCHWARDEN.

NORTH WILTS, *Feb.* 11, 1867.

LETTER VI.

DEAR SIR,—I have now to stand champion for the English Church, HER PURITY, free from the errors of *her sister* in Rome, and from what I conceive still worse, the "Heresy and Schism" that has existed *among us* from the Reformation to the present time.

It will be necessary, in order to show the working of our English Church system, to give some authority for the connexion of *the Church with the State*. I shall go back to the Jewish Church for example, first quoting the forty-ninth chapter of Isaiah, who, speaking of Christ being sent to the Gentiles, and the Church restored, says: "*And Kings shall be thy nursing fathers, and their Queens thy nursing mothers.*" It will be seen that *the Church*, by God's appointment, gives authority to Kings to rule! The first King given to the Jews was Saul; and we find Samuel officiating on the occasion. "Then *Samuel* took a vial of oil, and poured it upon his head, and kissed him, and said, Is it not because the Lord hath anointed thee to be captain *over his inheritance?*" In the case of David we find, "Therefore came all the elders of Israel to the King to Hebron, and David made a covenant with them in Hebron before the Lord, *and they anointed David King over Israel*, according to the word of the Lord by Samuel." Then with respect to Solomon; "And King David said, Call me Zadoc the priest, and Nathan the prophet; and the King said unto them, take with you the servants of the Lord, and cause Solomon my son to ride upon mine own mule, and bring him down to Gihon; *and let Zadoc the priest and Nathan the prophet* anoint him there King over Israel." Again: "*Elisha the prophet* called one of the children of the Prophets,' and sent him to Jehu to pour a box of oil on his head, and say, "Thus saith the Lord, I have anointed thee King over Israel." And King Solomon, too, fulfilled his office of *temporal head of the Church*, when he made that beautiful prayer at the dedication of the Temple. So it is with our English Sovereigns at their coronation; *the Archbishop of Canterbury, assisted by the Bishops*, officiate at the ceremony which makes the reigning Prince *the temporal head of the Church!!!*

We will now look to the Church of Rome, which I have entitled above "*Our Sister*," and which, at least for the *three first centuries*, till the reign of Constantine the Great, stood in the *front rank* of the Christian Churches, as doing honour to God by sending *four-fifths* of her Bishops and Popes into that assembly, which we recognize daily when we say, "THE NOBLE ARMY OF MARTYRS PRAISE THEE." Out of thirty Bishops and Popes of Rome that succeeded each other during the period from the Emperor Nero to Diocletian, and the ten persecutions in the reigns of the several Emperors of Rome, including those two, *there were but four that died a natural death*, TWENTY-FOUR SUFFERED MARTYRDOM, and two were slain. And if we look to St. Paul's Epistle to the Romans, chap. 1, ver. 8, he says, " First, I thank my God through Jesus Christ for you all, that *your* FAITH is spoken of *throughout the whole world*."

Whatever might be said in later years of the Popes of Rome being Antichrist, they, surely, were not during these three centuries. It was the Pagan Emperors during this period who filled that character—Domitian in the year eighty-seven, and Diocletian in 293, assuming the title of LORD and GOD, *and requiring their subjects to worship them as such.*

Here was no connexion of the Church and the State ; the Emperors were all Pagans, and we see the result. Our English Church (the Anglo-Saxon) although planted by St. Augustine, sent here by Pope Gregory, never became subject to Rome till the time of William the Conqueror, and his sons, William Rufus and Henry the First. The Conqueror *ruled by might*, and, consequently, was no " nursing father" to the Church. " After the death of Lanfranc, Archbishop of Canterbury, the see was left to the disposal of William Rufus, *who kept it open for four years while he plundered its revenues.* Other Bishoprics, Abbeys, and Priories, as they fell vacant, *he took in the same way into his own hands*"— (Churton's Early English Church). The reign of Henry the First was no better. " As to the Clergy, every parish church was put under a fine, *and the Parson was to pay a ransom for his liberty.*" Anselm, Archbishop of Canterbury, said to King Rufus (recognizing the Church and the State), " The Church is yours to defend and guard it as a patron ; it is not yours to invade its rights and lay it waste. It is the property of God, that His Ministers may live of it, not that your armies and wars should be supported from it "—(Ibid.).

It is not to be wondered at, that, treated as the Church was by these Norman conquerors, the Archbishop of Canterbury, William of Corboil, appealed to the Pope, Honorius II., who issued a bull appointing " our very dear brother, William, Archbishop of Canterbury, to the office of OUR VICAR *in England and Scotland.*"

This was the admission of Popery into our English Church. Had these Norman kings been " *the nursing fathers of the Church*," it might possibly never have happened ; as it was, it existed for 400 years, till the Reformation.

We will pass over this period, simply observing, that usurped power and might vested in one Church, and more especially *in one individual*, is certain to bring about abuses that in the end will undermine itself. So it was in our Church ; the worship of the Virgin Mary, the doctrine of Transubstantiation, of Purgatory, of works of supererogation, and a host of others, being followed up BY THE SALE OF INDULGENCES TO SIN, aroused the minds of our Reformers to the *iniquity of such a system*, and they, together with Henry VIII., of bull-dog courage, defied the Pope, and the reigning Prince again became " *the temporal head of the Church.*"

We have now to notice the unfortunate schisms and divisions that took place, where unity should have been the bond of love that moved them to action. On the accession of Queen Mary to the throne, the Reformers either became martyrs or exiles; the latter chiefly went over to Germany, among which number was John Jewel, afterwards BISHOP OF SALISBURY, and from his life, written by C. W. Le Bas, M.A., I gather the following information:—Jewel, having made the friendship of Peter Martyr, Professor of Divinity at Oxford, who had left the University and settled at Strasburg, went and resided with him in his exile, and here he was amongst his brethren in exile; but how different in mind and spirit the following quotation will prove:—" It is truly piteous to think that all these holy consolations" (the hope of returning home on the death of Queen Mary) "should ever have been overshadowed, even for a moment, by stormy contention among the Protestants themselves. But so, alas! it was. The demon of strife descended among the champions of peace and truth. The scenes of their banishment were converted into schools of angry controversy. In the first days of their exile the brethren, for the most part, dwelt together in unity; but many of them had, unhappily, sought refuge in various places where the genius of Calvin was predominant, and there they gradually imbibed a fondness and an admiration for the mighty works of that master builder of the tower of confusion. From that moment all concord and harmony was at an end among the exiled Protestants. The spirit of discord went forth from Geneva, and speedily shed its pernicious influence among the brethren at Frankfort. The English Liturgy was the first thing that suffered from the eruption. As early as 1554, the Reformers of Frankfort began to tamper with their service-book, and it soon appeared that the 'beginnings of strife are as when one letteth out water.' The proceedings of the malcontents were vehemently encouraged by John Knox, afterwards 'the great incendiary of Scotland;' and the effect of his interference was, that on the 15th of November, 1554, the men of Frankfort despatched to them of Zuric an open and bitter defiance of the English formularies. The men of Zuric retorted on the 28th of the same month; and, thenceforward, the debate became fierce and obstinate, and the breach well nigh incurable.

"It was in vain that Grindal and Chambers were sent from Strasburg for the purpose of allaying these commotions. It was equally in vain that representations were subsequently forwarded from the whole body of English at Strasburg, with the same pious and charitable object. These measures had no other effect but to drive the innovators to an appeal to the almost pontifical authority of Calvin. His decision, of course, was in favour of the dissentients; and they were thus confirmed in their bitter opposition to the English Ritual. In the following year (1555) some slight advantage was obtained over the Calvinistic party, by the exertions of Dr. Richard Cox, who arrived at Frankfort in March, and succeeded in driving Knox from the place, and re-establishing the Liturgy there. This success, however, was but transitory and insignificant. For in the ensuing August, Knox and Goodman retired to Geneva, the metropolis of schism, and were followed thither by the main body of the separatists. Under the ministry of these two men, they utterly rejected the whole scheme of the English Reformation, as accomplished in the reign of Edward VI., and professed their entire conformity to the discipline of Geneva. It is well known with what disastrous effect their principles were afterwards imported into England. At this period, Jewel was with Peter Martyr at Zuric, and no efforts were spared by him to heal these miserable distractions, and to bring back the spirit of peace and unity to the suffering Church. He omitted no topic of exhortation or entreaty which might recall them to a sense of their infatuation. But, alas! he was preaching to the tempest. The winds of discord had got loose ; and it far exceeded all human power to command them back to their confinement. They continued to rage with unabated fury, *and to render the Protestant cause, in the season of its adversity, a spectacle of sorrow to its most faithful followers,* AND OF EXULTATION *to its most malignant persecutors.*"

Here then at Geneva was the hot-bed, from whence those rank weeds, that were afterwards imported into England *and shore the Reformation of its glory,* were propagated ; but I am again trespassing too much on your space, and will conclude in another letter the further divisions at this time, with the consequences and effects to the present day.

I remain, dear Sir, yours truly,

A CHURCHWARDEN.

North Wilts, *March* 4, 1867.

LETTER VII.

To the Editor of the " Devizes Gazette."

Dear Sir,—My last letter concluded by showing how fearful were the divisions among the Reformers at Geneva ; and the English Divines who were exiled there returned in the reign of Elizabeth to instil the poison they had imbibed *into our Church system,* which required all the energy, *unity,* and zeal that could possibly be brought to bear, to grapple with the encroachments of Rome, and show the world at large that in reforming our Church they had no intention of upsetting or destroying the Catholic discipline therein, but to *thoroughly cleanse it* from every thing that was idolatrous, superstitious, or impure ! I will give another quotation from *Le Bas' Life of Jewel:*—" Another cause of confusion, which was then beginning to distract the kingdom—the scruples of the party since known by the title of *Puritans,* relative to the lawfulness of ceremonies and clerical attire, were beginning to assume a formidable shape ; and it was a most disastrous circumstance, that the cause of Nonconformity should find two leaders so distinguished by their learning and their piety as Sampson and Humphry. The names of such men gave incredible force to the insurrectionary movement which was then setting in against the authority and discipline of the Church, and which eventually effected the temporary downfall both of *the Altar and the Throne.* By these men, and men of the same stamp, *the true spirit of our Reformation appears to have been well-nigh forgotten.* It never was the intent of our original Reformers to present the Church of England to the public mind *under the aspect of a new establishment,* substituted in the place of an old one which had been subverted and demolished. The Church of England to which all their toils and cares were devoted WAS THE VERY SAME CHURCH WHICH HAD EXISTED FROM THE BEGINNING ; and their object was, not to sweep it from the face of the earth, and to plant another on its site ; *but to cleanse it from superstitious corruptions, and to effect its deliverance from a shameful servitude.* Unfortunately, however, many of our Protestant exiles brought back with them, from Geneva and Zuric, notions at mortal variance with the wisdom of our more moderate Reformers. They, too many of them, seemed to consider the Reformation as neither more nor less than the introduction of a totally new system, which should have nothing whatever in common with that which had passed away. Their imaginations were possessed with what they conceived to be the primitive model of Christian worship, every superficial relic of the former superstition was no better than an *accursed thing.* The surplice and the square cap were badges of the servitude which had been recently thrown off; and out of these prejudices and scruples had arisen a diversity of practice which was beginning to render the Reformation contemptible in the eyes of the public, and to afford an open triumph to the Papal party. The effect of all this dissention was unspeakably calamitous. Some forsook the Church because the habits were used ; others, again, because the habits were not used. All reasonable and sober-minded persons were disgusted at *the disorder which prevailed,* while the Romanist was loud in his denunciation of it, as at once the inevitable result and the righteous punishment of a national defection from the Apostolic unity.

Matters got even worse than this. One Cartwright, who was Margaret Professor of Divinity at Cambridge, went such lengths with the Puritans against the Church, that in 1571, the Houses of Convocation, together with the Parliament, took most stringent measures to bring the Nonconformists to reason. However much *dissention* might have prevailed in the English Church for the first eleven years of Queen Elizabeth's reign, *the sin of schism* was unknown. "Till about that time, 1570, the Roman Catholics held communion with the Reformed Church, and the Puritans the same. In 1569 Pius V. issued a bull in which he excommunicated Queen Elizabeth and her supporters. Those Roman Catholics who would not conform to the Reformation, now left the reformed Church and became a sect. The same year which witnessed the separation of the Romanists, was also the commencement of the Puritan separation. When they beheld the Reformation re-established according to the forms adopted in the reign of King Edward, they became dissatisfied; and after much fruitless agitation to alter the Church, they at length began to declaim against her as infected with Popish errors and superstitions; *and, affirming* EPISCOPACY *to be anti-Christian, they* SEPARATED *from the Church and formed conventicles,* about 1570. From this time the Puritans, *and those who followed their principles and practices* WITHOUT SEPARATING FROM THE CHURCH, became exceedingly troublesome.*"—Palmer's History of the Church.*

In my first letter, I said I would point out any *inconsistency* I might meet with in the task I had undertaken : here, then, was the commencement of that system which has existed ever since, and has *mistaught* millions of the Church's most earnest and zealous members. "Those who followed the principles and practices of the Puritans, *without separating from the Church"*—if the Bible is true, and those portions I have quoted from St. Paul's epistles, and the other writers in the New Testament have any meaning— have something to answer for *the consequences of their division.* The doctrine of the Low Church, *in opposition to Church principles,* has existed ever since. These men evidently feared the " sin of schism," and so kept within the communion of the Church ; but the effect of their teaching is too evident at the present time, when we see Churchmen deliberately asserting at a public meeting held at Dorchester, the following quotation, which I copy from your paper of February 28 :—" Lord Shaftesbury, in acknowledging the compliment [a vote of thanks as chairman] said Lord Portman had thrown out a suggestion of the greatest possible importance. His lordship had well said, that, if he was offended in his religious principles, and annoyed in one Church, he would go to another (*hear, hear*). He (Lord Shaftesbury) was not one who would hastily quit his parish Church, or the minister to whom he ordinarily listened ; but there were things paramount to that—loyalty to a pew was sometimes inconsistent with loyalty to Christ (*hear, hear*). He was therefore sure that, if Lord Portman's suggestion were carried into effect *with moderation and care,* it would produce the result they desired (*hear, hear*)." How can *the unity of the Church exist,* if these sentiments are cheered in a large assembly such as was held at Dorchester ?—and are they not *precisely the same* as those for which St. Paul rebuked the Corinthian Church ?—" I am of Paul, I of Apollos, I of Cephas, and I of Christ." Is CHRIST DIVIDED ? Well might Lord Shaftesbury recommend it should be done *" with moderation and care ;"* for who can tell, with such a system begun, where or how it would finish ? But we can come nearer home. Your paper of last week contains the account of a similar meeting at Devizes, where Mr. R. P. Long, one of the members for the Northern Division, attended to explain the formation of a Lay Association, where you report him to say :—" The Lay Association, however, would do, and he believed do effectively, that which was too invidious a thing for private individuals to undertake (*hear, hear*). Its promoters proposed, therefore, *if they succeeded in obtaining the adhesion of the greater part of the Churchwardens*, that in any case where the clergyman introduced practices and doctrines which hitherto had not been regarded as the practices and doctrines of the Church of England, the Churchwarden could call the attention of the Association to the matter. Then, after due inquiry, the Association would remonstrate with the Bishop ; and they hoped that such a remonstrance, proceeding from such a body, and backed up, as it would be, by the social influence of various members of the Church throughout the Diocese, *would have a weight with the Bishop which the remonstrance of a single individual perhaps might not have* (*hear, hear*). Such was the proposed *modus operandi*, and they believed it would be effectual. But, supposing they were mistaken, it would then devolve upon the Association to devise measures for getting over the difficulty in some other way. His hope, however, was, that the Bishop, of whom he wished to speak in the most respectful, reverential, and affectionate terms, would be influenced by the force of public opinion in the Diocese ; and that he would at once step forward and discharge what *they believed* was his duty at this critical juncture (*hear, hear*). But if his lordship refused to do so, they must then devise such measures as might be deemed expedient for obtaining that which they felt bound *to insist upon having* (*applause*), whether the Bishop was with or against them. They would not have their parish Churches spoiled. They would maintain, in their integrity, those services of the Church of England which they believed to be in accordance with her principles and her doctrines (*hear, hear*); and, whether the Bishop was with, or against them, from that point they would not swerve (*applause*). In the most temperate tone and manner they desired to make their remonstrance, *but give way they would not* (*applause*). And they were all the more resolute, because they desired to maintain a respectful, moderate, and reverential tone towards those in spiritual authority over them (*hear, hear*)."

I can truly sympathize with our worthy Bishop, and ask—Who would be a Bishop in these days ? He is answerable to God only for the manner in which he discharges his duty ; and yet we find him expected " to step forward and discharge what THEY *believed* was HIS duty at this critical juncture ! " And, moreover, if his lordship should consider it *his duty* not to interfere in certain cases where an individual Churchwarden may suppose the practices and doctrines exceeded those hitherto used in the Church of England (*which are of a very diverse character*), the Lay Association "would have a weight with the Bishop which the remonstrance of a single individual perhaps might not have." Is the Bishop then to have no liberty of conscience ? Is he supposed to be a mere tool, to work out the principles of a certain number of clergy, *who deny the spirituality of their holy office?* The honourable member, I trust, will excuse these remarks ; but, standing champion for our Church, I could do no otherwise than notice it.

There was a degree of consistency in those puritans who *left the Church of England* in the reign of Elizabeth ; but " *the Godly people"* went on in their hatred of the Church, till, with the Bible in one hand, and the sword in the other, the Altar and the Throne were attacked, and the Archbishop and the King were destroyed : those professing *extraordinary piety* overlooking that part of the Bible : " *Touch not mine anointed, and do my prophets no harm"!!*

Let us next look to Scotland. Where is the Church of God to be found there ? It is a very small, feeble, twinkling light ; but there it is, and always has been, "*the Episcopal Church.*" It is the only one that holds communion with our own ; but the State has ceased to be "*its nursing father.*" John Knox, of Geneva notoriety, whom Le Bas calls "'The great incendiary of Scotland," went there with his *anti-Episcopal notions,* and succeeded in instituting a NEW CHURCH ; one *free* from those restrictions which St. Paul left the first Bishop of the Cretians, in Crete, "*to set in order.*"

What has been the consequence ? By some means or other, the Holy Estate of Matrimony was performed edgeways ; and it was found that the high families in Scotland were illegitimate, and an Act of Parliament had to be passed to legalize the same. There was nothing of this in the Episcopal Church ; and so it happens that those who will run counter to the Apostolic rule, bring about circumstances not very favourable to themselves.

One of the effects of the divisions in the English Church is seen, in the State having legalized what used to be the "Holy Estate of Matrimony" *into a civil contract.* Think of this !—the Almighty first said, " Therefore shall a man leave his father and mother and cleave unto his wife, *and they twain shall be one flesh.*" Our Saviour, in alluding to it, says, " *What God has joined together,* let no man put asunder." And St. Paul, in the 5th chapter of the Ephesians, likens the married state *to Christ and His Church;* and concludes, " For this cause shall a man leave his father and his mother and shall be joined unto his wife, and *they shall be one flesh. This is a great mystery;* but I speak concerning Christ and the Church." If any of those parties *married at the Board of Guardians,* or the like, should come to inherit property, their marriage will not be disputed in law ; *but that* GOD *has had any thing to do with such a ceremony,* it is absurd to think of. And how can *His blessing* be expected on those who choose to make such *an agreement?* There is none of that "*mystical union*" spoken of by St. Paul, and consequently we may conclude *they are twain still!!!*

The quotations I have made have so lengthened my letter, that, as I wish to notice the Irish Church, and the purity of our own, I will conclude this.

Remaining yours truly,

A CHURCHWARDEN.

LETTER VIII.

To the Editor of the "Devizes Gazette."

DEAR SIR,—I have now to notice the Church in Ireland, planted by St. Patrick in the year 432, and continued free from the aggressions of Rome till the twelfth century. At the Reformation, in the reign of Elizabeth, it rejected the Papal power, and the English ritual was again introduced. Two Bishops only, out of about twenty-six, refused to agree with the Reformation, *and were driven from their sees.* Here is another instance of the Church REMAINING THE SAME, *but cleansed from her errors;* but we have to notice the anomaly of two Episcopal Churches (*if such can possibly exist*)—the Irish Catholic Church, and *the Roman Catholic Church in Ireland.* Can any one doubt which is the true Church there? Is God the author of confusion? Or is it likely that He who, by the mouth of His Prophet Samuel, says, "That rebellion is as the sin of witchcraft;" and, by St. Paul, "That whosoever resisteth the higher powers, resisteth the ordinances of God, and shall receive to himself damnation"—could ever sanction the perpetual rebellions that the Popes of Rome have instigated (Pius V. and Gregory XIII., in particular), to force the Irish people into the Romish Communion again.

Pius V. conferred the dominions of the Queen to Philip II., King of Spain! Gregory XIII. issued a bull, in which all who should unite *in rebellion against Queen Elizabeth* were promised *a plenary pardon of their sins!*

But I can best illustrate the fearful consequences of this schism by a quotation from Palmer's "History of the Church."

"It was only by a long series of rebellions that the schism in Ireland was consolidated, and became so widely extended. The reign of Queen Elizabeth, however, sufficed for this lamentable catastrophe. King James I. wisely discouraged the Roman schism, *and forbade the residence of its Bishops, Priests and Jesuits in his dominions;* but, under his successor, Charles I., a relaxation of this wholesome severity encouraged the Schismatics in Ireland to insult and disturb the Church; and ultimately, in 1641, to massacre in cold blood a hundred and fifty thousand of its adherents, and to break into insurrection.

"The Church was now dreadfully persecuted by the Papists and by the English Parliament; but, on the return of Charles II., resumed its rights. Persecution was renewed under James II., in 1690, when the Romish party obtained power; and in the rebellion of 1798. From that period, the Romish party has acquired great political power, and the Church has been almost continually persecuted, especially within the last few years, in which the clergy have been reduced nearly to starvation; some have been murdered, and many placed in peril of their lives. To add to their afflictions, *the Government,* in 1833, *suppressed ten of the*

Bishoprics, on pretence of requiring their revenues for the support of ecclesiastical buildings ; although the Bishops of Ireland, in a body, protested against such an act ; and offered to pay the amount required from the income of their sees, provided that *so great an injury* were not done to the cause of religion."

We see here the fearful consequence of such *a schism as the Church of Rome, which is in Ireland;* and the sooner the world can be satisfied that the ONE *Episcopal Church* WHICH HAS BEEN, or is to be found, in nearly all the nations of the earth, IS THE TRUE CHURCH OF GOD, the better and the happier it will be for all parties.

We are told, and I have noticed above, "that the Almighty is not the author of confusion." It was the Devil that caused our first parents to sin ! It was he that withstood the Almighty to His face, and told Him that holy Job would deny Him, if he was only afflicted ! It was he who had the audacity to tempt our blessed Saviour in the wilderness; and, if possible, to frustrate the salvation of mankind !

It is he that has caused all the heresies, schisms, and divisions in God's Church!—and it is he, still, that blinds the eyes of men, that they should not see *the effects* of the multitude of opinions they hold till it is too late, till that which has been (which I will conclude this letter with) may perhaps be again : and Christianity itself, which *a laxity* of opinion *and Church principles* may undermine, give way (as it has done before) TO INFIDELITY.

Let us now look and see if there is any *real cause* for these divisions. I will take the life of a man, from his birth to his death in old age ; first quoting the words of our Saviour, *when giving authority to the eleven Apostles,* "Go YE into all the world, and preach the Gospel *to every creature.* He that believeth *and is baptized* shall be saved ; but he that believeth not shall be damned."

Our Church, then, finding these *the terms of man's salvation,* when an infant is born, calls him into her Communion by baptism, *that the original sin of Adam* which he inherited by nature may be *"washed away,"* and that he who was " born in wrath" may become the child of God ! Here she takes a merciful part ; for if, as some assert, persons ought not to be baptized till they are adults and penitents,— if they should die at any time *unbaptized,* there is no assurance of their salvation ; and the rubric of our burial service says it is not to be read over such persons, plainly showing the opinion of those who compiled it. Having taken surety of *the faith* of sponsors, that the child shall be taught " the Creed, the Lord's Prayer, and the Ten Commandments," she next calls upon him to ratify in his own person, at Confirmation, what he could not do in infancy, and to acknowledge himself bound to believe what his sponsors had promised for him !

The Church, too, has compiled a Catechism for his instruction, in which she explains *her meaning* of those things he is to believe : she has also a service for private baptism, *and also for adults.* And the mother is not forgotten ; there is a service for her to attend, and offer her thanks *and offerings* (like the Virgin Mary of old) for her safe delivery! Alas! that dissent should ever have been the cause of making people forget the *true reason* why that offering is made. Yet I know an instance in my own parish (the man told me himself), that he had taken his wife to the Methodist Chapel in the next parish to have her "Churched;" for he did not see why he should pay a shilling at the Church when he could get it *done* at the Chapel *for nothing!!*

The Christian next inclines to the married state. The Church is provided with a service *after the law of God;* and there is no question but "they twain are made one flesh." Her bells, too, rejoice with the happy pair :—

> " Oh, merry are the village bells
> That sound with soothing chime
> From the dim old tower, *grown grey beneath*
> *The shadowy touch of time ;*
> And gaily are they borne along
> Upon the summer air,
> *Telling of bridal happiness*
> To the youthful and the fair."

Those bells, too, call him weekly, and, in many instances, daily, to worship and service :—

> " 'Tis past, the bridal glee is past,
> Those echoing peals are o'er ;
> But the sweet, the Holy Sabbath comes,
> We hear them now once more,
> With a message from the heaven of love,
> *A voice that speaks to all ;*
> Unto the temple of our God,
> Unto His shrine THEY CALL."

And again, when he dies, they call him to his last home, to await the day of the general resurrection !—

> " And yet once more your music breaks
> Upon my listening ear,
> Though not the gaily-sounding notes
> We love so well to hear ;
> Changed is your message to the heart,
> Your joyous tone is fled ;
> You speak to us of buried hopes,
> A requiem of the dead."

But ere that takes place in old age, he has a lifetime to pass: " to work out his own salvation with fear and trembling." His Church takes care he shall not be ignorant (*unless wilfully so*) of all it is necessary he should know. She does what she can to teach him to read the Scriptures, but she provides that all may know them *by hearing*, if they will only attend her service; for she appoints to go through the whole of the Bible and Testament during the year, and the principal chapters on Sundays and Holy Days. Her prayers and supplications, too, are after the manner given by St. Paul to Timothy and Titus.

She has given us a Creed also, compiled by the Apostles themselves, that we may not be ignorant of what is essential that all should know; and, that all believing *the same*, there may be that *Unity* in the Church that the Bible teaches; and when the Church was beset with heresy in the days of Arius, 318 bishops assembled at the Council of Nice, condemned his heresy, and established the Nicene Creed, further to instruct and keep in the true faith the members of the Universal or Catholic Church; and, after that, the Creed of St. Athanasius was added, to explain, as far as we are permitted to know, the mystery of the Holy Trinity!

Our Churchman occasionally falls sick, in old age, perhaps "unto death." He is instructed "To call for *the elders of the Church*, and let them pray over him. *And the prayer of faith shall save the sick, and the Lord shall raise him up; and if he has committed sins, they shall be forgiven him.*" The time approaches that he must die. She calls him to his last home to rest around her sacred walls, till the trumpet shall sound at the general resurrection. Nothing can be more beautiful or sublime than her service here: she hails his remains with the cheering words, " I am the resurrection and the life, saith the Lord: he that believeth in Me, though he were dead, *yet shall he live;* and whosoever liveth and believeth in Me, *shall never die.*" We are told, in the lesson, that that body about to be sown " *is not quickened* EXCEPT IT DIE," and then we commit his body to the ground (from whence it was taken) "earth to earth, ashes to ashes, dust to dust; in sure and certain hope of THE RESURRECTION to eternal life, through our Lord Jesus Christ."

What more on earth can a Christian require than this? Our Church used, in days of old, to be called " The Poor Man's Church." Is it so in the present day? I fear not: the *divisions* among her own clergy, the different sects that have risen up among us, " *drawing away disciples after them,* AS ST. PAUL PREDICTED: the propagating a slang, vulgar term invented by Satan himself, " The nearer the Church, the further from God." All this has so alienated the peasantry of England from their parish churches, that if we go on as at present, there will be no need after a time to go abroad to convert the heathen.

Then again, look at her parochial system! In every parish there is a regularly ordained minister, licensed by his bishop to the cure of that parish; *and, whether the inhabitants will receive him or not,* it must not be forgotten, the sentence our Saviour passed on all those who would not receive and hear the twelve apostles and seventy disciples he sent out by twos into every city. On the other hand, the words of the Prophet Ezekiel apply to him: " So thou, O son of man, I have set thee a watchman unto the house of Israel; therefore thou shalt hear the word at My mouth, and warn them from Me. When I say unto the wicked, O wicked man, thou shalt surely die; if thou *dost not speak* to warn the wicked from his way, that wicked man shall die in his iniquity, BUT HIS BLOOD *will I require at thine hand.*"

I find I am again taking too much of your space, so I must make one more letter to notice those of our clergy who have taken up

the ritualistic movement, and the consequences of division to
the Churches of the East by *their divisions*, and the sword of
Mahomet.

I remain, dear Sir, yours faithfully,

A CHURCHWARDEN.

North Wilts, *Easter*, 1867.

LETTER IX.

To the Editor of the " Devizes Gazette."

Dear Sir,—In concluding this series of letters on the Christian
Church, it remains to notice that portion of our Clergy who have
caused such *a stir* of late among those who form the low Church
and the Dissenters. Those men who advocate high ritualistic
practices.

I can say much in their favour, and a great deal against them.
The Church Union they advocate must *in principle* be a sound
measure : St. Paul's epistles (that I have so fully quoted) are full
of it : it is not the scant measure of union in our own Church only,
though we have much to do here ; but union, sooner or later, with
all the Churches in the world, *Rome included ! ! !*

If the *peaceable* Kingdom of Christ shall ever happen—if " the
wolf shall dwell with the lamb, and the leopard lie down with
the kid "—if " He shall a second time assemble the outcasts of
Israel from the four corners of the earth "—and, " *the envy* of
Ephraim *shall depart*, and the adversaries of Judah shall be cut
off : Ephraim shall not *envy* Judah, and Judah shall not vex
Ephraim,"—should this happen in this generation, and Christ's
" Kingdom come," how would those persons stand reproved and
convicted who are for ever crying out, " No peace with Rome."
The Church of Rome is our sister ; it is true she is an erring one,
but that is the very reason why we should try to reclaim her. An
offer (if I am not mistaken) has been tendered to her to hold communion with us, upon *true* Catholic principles ; she contemptuously
rejected it—saying, it was for us to repent of the heresies and
schisms we had been guilty of, and then return to the true Church.
This is nothing more than we could expect. Can Rome (*who is
united in herself*) look upon *the divisions* in our Church with any
other view than she did at the Reformation ? Even if she were
inclined to admit her errors, could she not reply, on application for
reunion : " First cast out the beam that is *in thine own eye*, and then
shalt thou *see clearly* to cast out the mote that is in thy brother's
eye ? " The principle of " Church Union " is correct : would that
those who advocate it would show *their sincerity* by following
the example of St. Paul, who says, " All things are lawful for me,
but all things are not expedient ! " The Ritualists strangely outdo
St. Paul, for all things they do are *not lawful !* Witness the

incense, and the elevation of the consecrated elements for adoration—and, again, having promised at their ordination "*reverently to obey their ordinary* and other chief ministers," they appear to have forgotten that part of a Christian minister's duty. But even supposing they were right so far, surely *it is not expedient*, the extreme part they are taking. Our *Reformed Church* requires nothing more than that the Priest should wear the white surplice, "*the emblem of purity*," externally ; and, as regards the inner man, "*let your Priests be clothed with righteousness.*" It is true, in the Jewish Church, the Lord commanded Moses " to make holy garments for Aaron and his sons, *for glory and for beauty; and* to make them "of gold, and blue, and purple, and scarlet, and fine linen." Yet we find John the Baptist, who was sent to prepare the way for the Saviour and the Christian Church, "*had his raiment of camel's hair*, and a leathern girdle about his loins :" showing, at all events, there is no necessity for keeping up the Jewish custom in the Christian Church ! And, moreover, if *unity* is their object, how much sooner would they gain *the laity* over to them, if to the zeal with which they labour for their flocks (which even Dissenters give them credit for) they had the discretion to know what things " *were not expedient.*"

I have now given what I believe to be a Scriptural view of " what constitutes a Church." Would that those who differ from her would *in time* consider what possibly might be the effect in our own England of the multitude of opinions that her people *choose to hold*—yea, consider whether the words of Jeremiah may possibly apply to us : " Shall I not visit for these things, saith the Lord ? Shall not my soul be avenged *on such a nation as this?* A wonderful and horrible thing is committed in the land. The Prophets *prophesy falsely*, and the Priests bear rule by their means, *and My people love to have it so*—and what will ye do in the end thereof?"

What has been done in the end thereof, where other nations, *slighting the privilege of the Christian Church among them*, have had their candlesticks removed, I will show, by again quoting "Palmer's History of the Church."

" While the Monothelite heresy was disturbing the Church, the false prophet Mahomet and his followers were conquering the Asiatic possessions of the Eastern Empire, and extending their triumphs through Egypt, and along the northern coast of Africa. Mahomet was an impostor whose pretensions would have sunk into immediate obscurity, like those of many other pretended Prophets, had they not been sustained *by force of arms* and vast military success. He declared that a Divine commission had been given to him to establish the true religion *by force of arms*, and to destroy idolatry. He admitted that the Jewish and the Christian revelations were Divine ; but he pretended that they were only introductory to his own ; and while he denounced eternal damnation to those who should refuse to receive it, he forced them *at the point of the sword* to take the alternative of *slavery or death*.

" In Egypt and the East, the invaders were assisted by the Eutychian and Nestorian heretics ; and their religion consequently

received a degree of favour which was denied to that of the
Church. Persecution at length assailed the faith of Christians ;
and the result was, that in Africa, after four or five centuries, *we
hear no more of those four or five hundred episcopal sees* which had
formerly shed light on that region. In the East, Christianity
slowly declined under oppression and persecution ; but it was
always preserved ; and, after the lapse of twelve hundred years,
there are still many Churches in Asia Minor, Syria, Palestine, and
Egypt, *though they bear but a small proportion to the eight hundred
episcopal Churches which, in the fifth century, existed in those
countries.*

" It would be in vain for us to attempt to fathom the profound
depths of those Divine counsels which permitted so large a portion
of Christianity to pine away and perish beneath the yoke of
Mohammedan infidelity. What may be the final ends and objects
of this visitation, are at present concealed from our view ; *but some
lessons it does distinctly convey.* The Nestorians and Eutychians of
the East had revolted against the truth of the Gospel, and arro-
gantly despised the united judgments of the whole Christian world.
The Donatists in Africa had separated from their Christian brethren, and by violence and bloodshed had established *their human
Church.* In all those countries which Mohammedanism perma-
nently subjugated, *schism and heresy* had struck deep roots, and
obtained many adherents. The separatists made common cause
with the infidels, and rejoiced to see the Church oppressed, *but
they brought destruction on themselves.* All were involved in a
common ruin ; and those who had rejected the truth, as well as
those who retained it, were delivered over to the tyranny and the
degradation of the infidel dominion. How great must have been
those offences, and how odious in the sight of God, which brought
down so terrible a punishment on these nations, involving even
the Church of God in their calamities ! And may we not most
justly fear, *lest nations* in which similar offences extensively and
long prevail, may be delivered over to judgments equally awful,
and deprived of those means of grace and that way of salvation
which so many of them have despised and rejected ?

" Such examples should furnish new arguments against *volun-
tary separation* from the Church of Christ."

Here is indeed a lesson, if Englishmen will only learn it. As
Nadab, and Abihu, and Korah, Dathan, and Abiram, and all that
belonged to them, were destroyed for their schism, division, and
rebellion in the Jewish Church, by the direct hand of God, so was
Mahomet *permitted* by Him to destroy the *Christian faith* in those
nations in the East and West, where many of " the prophets pro-
phesied falsely, and God's people *loved to have it so.*" " Shall
not my soul be avenged on such a nation as this ?"

Where, at the present time, are the Seven Churches of Asia ?
The " false prophet" can answer for what has become of them. Six
of them, at least, he has destroyed—as regards Smyrna, of whom
St. John writes to the angel, or messenger, or bishop : " These
things saith the first and the last, which was dead and is alive ; I

know thy works, and tribulation, and poverty (*but thou art rich*), be thou faithful unto death, and I will give thee a crown of life." As regards Smyrna, Dr. Walsh, who was chaplain to the English Embassy at Constantinople, in 1838, writes : "The approach to Smyrna was very enlivening. Of all the cities of the Apocalpyse, this is the only one *which is not desolate.* There was no denunciation of the removal of its candlestick, like that of Ephesus; and it is now, perhaps, as populous and flourishing as it was in the time of the Apostles." Still it was under Turkish government, and the Church existing in a climate of infidelity.

He speaks, too, of having visited the ancient city of Nice, or Nicæa, its walls eight miles in circumference, twenty-five feet high, and fourteen feet thick at the base, and then in a state of perfection, though not a vestige of a street or a building was to be seen inside the whole town, except one solitary Greek family. The sword of Mahomet had destroyed the place where formerly was held the grand synod; where 318 bishops, besides a vast crowd of Presbyters and deacons were summoned by the Emperor Constantine, and assembled to condemn the Arian heresy, and from whence we derived the Nicene Creed.

He gives the following graphic description of the place :— "From the time of those important Councils, Nicæa continued to be, not only a celebrated, but also a large and populous city . . . . Even so late as the year 1677, it was a flourishing and populous town. It then contained a population of 10,000 Christian Greeks, and many precious remains of antiquity to attest its former splendour. But the desolating hand of the Turks has since effaced every trace of this, and it is a subject of melancholy contemplation now to behold it, the shadowy phantom of a magnificent city, on a beautiful and fertile spot, where bountiful nature has provided every thing necessary for human life ; an extensive plain exuberant with fertility, sloping lawns verdant with pasture, wooded hills covered with the finest timber, expanding waters teeming with fish, and a climate the most bland and delicious that ever refreshed a mortal frame. Yet here *human life is actually extinguished,* human habitations *totally obliterated,* and the solitude rendered more striking by the irrefragable testimonies of its former splendour, and the visible evidences of what it recently was, and what it still might be."

These two cities of Smyrna and Nicæa teach us again another lesson ! St. Polycarp, the pupil of the Apostle St. John, and who was ordained by him Bishop of Smyrna, was the individual whom St. John addressed in the Revelation as " the Angel of the Church of Smyrna;" and to whom he says (speaking in the person of the Saviour), " Be thou faithful unto death, and I will give thee a crown of life." St. Polycarp, after ministering eighty-six years, received the crown of martyrdom in the year 167, under the reign of Marcus Aurelius, being burnt alive in the hundredth year of his age ! Who can tell but that the veneration and respect in which he was held for his piety, and " faithfulness unto death," was the means of *salting* the city of Smyrna to the present time ; as our

Saviour said to his Apostles, " Ye are salt of the earth?" On the other hand, let us contrast the conduct of Theognis, Bishop of Nice, who, at the time the great Council was held, was strongly imbued with the Arian heresy, and who, although he subscribed his name to the Nicene Creed, was still unconvinced by the multitudes of proofs brought against the heretic Arius. Only three months after the Council had dispersed, he went to the Emperor Constantine with Eusebius, another bishop, and told him " We have done ill, Sir, in that, for fear of you, *we have subscribed an* IMPIOUS CONFESSION." Here, "*the salt had lost its savour*;" and, may be, the *poison he instilled* never ceased to exist in the city of Nicæa, till the sword of Mahomet was permitted to do its dreadful work ! ! !

Let us for a moment consider what these champions for the truth had to do at this first general Council at Nice. There were no railways in those days, and no steam ships that can cross the Atlantic, 2000 miles, in nine days. Yet the Emperor cited bishops from all parts of the known world at that time—from Europe, Asia, and Africa ; and 318 attended, besides a host of Presbyters and deacons. They were taken by the public conveyances at the Emperor's charge, and he maintained them during upwards of two months that the Council sat ! ! !

If any thing be wanting to prove "*what constitutes a Church*," surely, here it is ! Here is the Catholic, or universal Church, assembled together to protect the faith. And could one be held in the present day in our own country ? What part could the Wesleyans, the Calvinists, the Unitarians, the Independents, and all the other sects, take at such an assembly ?

In conclusion, I have one word to say with respect to the term " Protestant." No man is more ready than myself to protest against the errors of the Church of Rome ; but, unfortunately, many members of the English Church have substituted the term for the word Catholic : the effect of which is, *they have forfeited their birthright*, and the *Roman* Catholics must laugh in their sleeves to think that, when *we* speak of " *the Catholics*," we mean them ! The Apostles' Creed, given to the Church *in its earliest days*, teaches us to believe in " the Holy *Catholic* Church !" The *Nicene Creed*, composed by Hosius at the Council of Nice, and subscribed by all the Bishops there assembled, instructs us to say, " I believe in one Catholic and Apostolic Church," and the Creed of St. Athanasius tells us, " Whosoever will be saved, before all things *it is necessary* that he hold the *Catholic* faith." And the *Catholic* faith is this, that we worship one God in Trinity, and Trinity in Unity." Then again, " So are we forbidden by the *Catholic* religion to say, There be three Gods, or three Lords." And it concludes, " This is the *Catholic faith*, which, except a man believe faithfully, he cannot be saved."

The term "*Protestant*" is not to be found in the *Bible, the Testament, or the Prayer Book.* And, if it were *possible* that we could be a *Protestant Church, apart* from the *Catholic* or universal Church of Christ (a mere thing of *human invention*), we should become a pretty spectacle to " angels and to men."

No; let us not be any longer misled by this term. *Protest*, if you like; but take care that we don't yield to Rome the *privilege* of being considered *members of the Catholic Church*.

I have now to thank you for the patience you have shown, and the space you have afforded me in your valuable paper; and I trust that the Scripture quotations I have made will satisfy some, at least, that our Saviour, when He instituted the Christian Church, and prayed, as He did to His heavenly Father, "that they may be *one*, even as He and His Father were one," never intended to be worshipped in the multitude of ways at present to be met with, and any other, that any PRIVATE INDIVIDUAL may set up for himself.

I remain, dear Sir, yours truly,

A CHURCHWARDEN.

NORTH WILTS, *May* 13, 1867.

LETTER TO THE REV. LORD SIDNEY G. OSBORNE.

To the Editor of the " Devizes Gazette."

DEAR SIR,—The following letter I have sent to the *Times*, as the patron of the Rev. S. G. O., supposing they would have the candour and honesty to give it insertion in their columns. As they have not given it publicity, I presume they wish to keep the principles held by the rev. lord intact, and allow the serious charge he has made against our worthy Bishop to have its full effect with their readers.

As an advocate for the truth, I beg its insertion in your paper:—

To the Rev. Lord S. G. Osborne.

My LORD,— I have just received officially from "the Salisbury Diocesan Church Lay Association," as one of the Churchwardens of this parish, a copy of your letter to the Lord Bishop of the Diocese, which appeared in the *Times* some time since.

As a private individual, I should not have presumed to have noticed any part of that letter; but as the Lay Association have an object to serve in publishing and circulating it among the Churchwardens; as one of them, I trust you will allow me to be as outspoken as yourself, and see whether the doctrines you repudiate and our Bishop maintains, are those our Church established at the Reformation, when she compiled her Prayer Book."

This is a serious subject; as, in your letter, you boldly imply that the Bishop ought not to hold the holy office he does; or otherwise, "could you be convinced" the doctrines he has put forward in his

charge " were those of our Church, you would not remain in connexion with her."

In the fourth paragraph of your letter you utterly repudiate, as
the doctrine of the Church, the real presence in the consecrated
elements of the Holy Eucharist, and the power of the Priesthood to
pardon or retain sins, which the Bishop insisted on in his charge.

In the fifth paragraph " you deny that the clergy, through their
ordination, are invested with any prerogative purely Divine, either
in regard to any action on the elements of the Lord's Supper, or
in giving or withholding absolution from sin."

In the sixth paragraph, you solemnly assert *your disbelief* " that
any rational interpretation of the Scripture would justify you in
teaching your people that, by any operation at your hands, the
bread and wine can become the channel of an ineffable mystery, in
the sense that inwardly it becomes ' that which my Saviour took
from the blessed Virgin, which He offered on the cross as a
sacrifice.' "

Now, my lord, permit me to ask you, with regard to the *teaching*
of your parishioners, if the children in your parish are taught the
Church Catechism ?—because therein you are teaching this very
principle !—" What is the outward part or sign of the Lord's
Supper ?—" Bread and wine, which the Lord hath commanded to
be received." " What is the inward part or thing signified ?"—
" The *body and blood of Christ*, which are *verily and indeed taken
and received* by the faithful in the Lord's Supper."

This is how the Church instructs her children; and her Twenty-
eighth Article says, " *The Body of Christ is given, taken*, and *eaten*
in the Supper, only after an heavenly and spiritual manner." And
again, in the prayer before consecrating the elements, *you* pray
the Almighty, " That He will grant us grace so to eat the flesh of
Thy dear Son Jesus Christ, and drink His blood, that our sinful
bodies *may be made clean* by *His body*, and *our souls washed* through
His most precious *blood*," &c. And in the prayer of consecration,
you say, " Hear us, O merciful Father, we most humbly beseech
Thee, and grant that we, receiving these Thy creatures of bread
and wine, according to Thy Son our Saviour Jesus Christ's holy
institution, in remembrance of His death and passion, may be *partakers of* His most blessed *body* and *blood*."

Our Church, too, is authorized in asserting this by our Saviour
Himself, who said, on instituting the Holy Supper, " Take, eat, *this*
is *my body*," " Drink ye all of this, *for this* is *my blood*."

There can be no question that the Church always held this
doctrine, though unfortunately her ministers have seldom or never
taught it ; and the natural consequence is, so many of the laity are
inclined to disbelieve it, and have taken the part they have done
against the Bishop. As her Twenty-eighth Article asserts, " The
body of Christ is given, taken, and eaten, in the Supper, *only* after
an *heavenly* and *spiritual* manner." There is, therefore, no analogy
(as you say) between that and the transubstantiation, or the *carnal
presence*, held by the Church of Rome.

With respect to your denial " That the clergy have any power invested in them in giving or withholding absolution," I have been writing for several months past in the *Devizes Gazette* a series of letters on the Christian Church. My arguments were controverted by a clergyman in North Wilts; and I replied to him in the following words—which, substituting your own parish for the one in question, will well apply to your lordship:—

"I like to illustrate these things, if possible; so will fancy myself a parishioner of Durweston, one who had led a bad life, like 'the thief on the cross;' and like him, too, shown mercy at the eleventh hour. On my death bed, I become a true penitent; and read in St. James, 'If any be sick among you, let him call for the elders of the Church, and let them pray over him: and the prayer of faith shall save the sick, and the Lord shall raise him up; and if he has committed sins, *they shall be forgiven him.*' Accordingly, I send for your lordship, my pastor: you attend me, and, according to the instructions of *your Church*, you read to me the service 'for the visitation of the sick.' When, after acknowledging my faith, and expressing repentance of my past life, *you* are authorized to administer to me *the absolution*, which differs from the general absolution, 'He (the Almighty) pardoneth and absolveth;' or from the absolution in the Communion Service, 'Almighty God, our heavenly Father, have mercy upon you—pardon and deliver you from all your sins,' &c. But in this case, YOU, my lord, address me as follows:—'Our Lord Jesus Christ, *who hath left power to His Church* TO ABSOLVE all sinners who truly repent and believe in Him, of His great mercy forgive thee thine offences; and by *His authority* COMMITTED TO ME, I ABSOLVE *thee from all thy sins*, in the name of the Father, and of the Son, and of the Holy Ghost.' What great comfort this to the *dying penitent!* it sounds like the gracious words of our Saviour, 'This day thou shalt be with Me in paradise.'"

You admit, in the fifth paragraph, "you have authority to declare to the congregation that, when penitent, their sins are remitted; JUST *as you have the same authority* to make any one declaration, which concerns the statement to them, of any one simple truth of the Gospel."

Now our Church certainly does not limit the office of the Priest to so low an ebb as you have stated above, for if such were the fact, you would have been allowed when *a deacon* to have *read the absolution* "the same as you could declare the truths of the Gospel." But you know perfectly well that, as a deacon, you were not allowed to read the absolution, or to *consecrate* the elements at the Holy Communion.

Well, my lord, *you* applied for Priest's orders; and what *authority* did you receive? After promising reverently to obey your ordinary and other chief ministers, and many other questions, the Church requires an answer to—"the Bishop and Priests present laid their hands on you; the Bishop saying, 'Receive the Holy Ghost for the office and work of a Priest in the Church of God,'" &c. "Whose sins THOU *dost forgive, they are forgiven*; and whose sins THOU *dost retain, they are retained.*"

Can you, my lord, doubt the power given to you at your ordination; or is this service a mere farce? When our Saviour had done every thing necessary to man's salvation, and had paid the penalty for sin by His death, there was one thing He had *not done*, and He came on earth again and *gave authority* to His eleven apostles *in the very words you received yours!* And He promised to be with them always, "*even to the end of the world.*" This must include yourself as well as them, from whom you have derived your own.

There is one instance in the Bible of the "retaining of sins," (which the Bishop mentioned in his charge). St. Paul, who most probably received ordination from the Apostles themselves, in writing to Timothy, says, that Hymenius and Alexander, having made *shipwreck of the faith*, "he had delivered *unto Satan*, that they might learn not to blaspheme;" or, in other words, he had *excommunicated them* from the Church.

You say, in the ninth paragraph, "I am one of those who think that, allowing a great margin for private opinion, there is a limit at which none are justified in holding office in an Establishment recognized as Protestant. If, passing that limit, they avow a creed repugnant to every idea connected with the history of our Church, her preaching and practice for centuries, I esteem them not justified, for their own sake, or for the sake of those who are true to her, to remain within her pale."

These are strong words, my lord, and seem to imply that our Bishop ought not to continue to fill the office he does. You conclude by saying, "Could I be brought to believe the doctrines on which I have now commented to be those of our Church, I would not remain in connection with her."

The simple mode I have adopted, by supposing myself to be one of your parishioners, to illustrate our Church's teaching; and the services I have quoted—to my mind, distinctly prove that the charge of our Bishop is *strictly in keeping with the doctrine of the Church.* Should you be able *to prove* that I am wrong, I shall be quite ready to apologize to your lordship for having presumed to venture on a subject too deep for my comprehension; at the same time, I am satisfied, till such proof is given, that if one of the two, the Bishop or yourself (according to your own argument), ought to leave the Church, it might be decided in the words of the Prophet Nathan to David.

I remain, my lord, with all due respect,

Your faithful servant,

J. A. WILLIAMS,
One of the Churchwardens of the Parish of Baydon,
North Wilts.

June 11, 1867.

TO THE CHURCHWARDENS OF THE DIOCESE OF SARUM.

GENTLEMEN,—All of you that were present at the meeting of the Lay Association at Salisbury, on Tuesday last, are aware that I could obtain no hearing to explain why I could not agree with a large number of yourselves, in condemning the charge of our Bishop "as having a tendency to the Romish doctrine of transubstantiation." I therefore ask of you patiently to go through my arguments, free from prejudice or bigotry. Answer me, any of you, if you think I am wrong; and let us look at this *serious charge* with that Christian spirit and with that charity which should guide the proceedings of such a large number of influential persons who are entrusted with the temporal management of our Churches.

When the programme of the Association was sent to me, I thought of becoming a member : *its very title* gave it an authority in my mind, that it was just what was required in the English Church.

It was as follows :—

"The Lay Association of *Members of the Church of England*, in the Diocese of Salisbury, FOR UPHOLDING THE PRINCIPLES OF THE ESTABLISHED CHURCH."

Now, I am free to admit that *the above title* would ensure my membership, *and all my energy* in support of such an Association ; but how I was confounded and thrown aback, when, on reading in the *Devizes Gazette* the account of a meeting at Devizes to inaugurate the said Society, Mr. Long, the honourable member for the Northern Division of our county, gave utterance to such sentiments with respect to the Bishop of the Diocese, that I was convinced *the Association* did not intend to perform *what it professed to do*—"To uphold the principles of the Established Church."

Now, my object in going to Salisbury was to ask of the meeting, *what were the principles of the Church of England*, and where are they to be found ?

There is no question but they are to be found in "the Book of Common Prayer"; and the question next arises—by whom was that Prayer Book compiled ?

It was compiled by DR. CRANMER, Archbishop of Canterbury. Six Bishops : viz., Dr. Goodrich, Bishop of Ely; Dr. Skip, Bishop of Hereford ; Dr. Thirlby, Bishop of Westminster ; Dr. Day, Bishop of Chichester ; Dr. Holbeck, Bishop of Lincoln ; Dr. RIDLEY, Bishop of Rochester. Four Deans : viz., Dr. May, Dean of St. Paul's ; Dr. Taylor, Dean of Lincoln ; Dr. Heynes, Dean of Exeter ; Dr. Redman, Dean of Westminster. Dr. Cox, King Edward's Almoner ; and Dr. M. Robinson, Archdeacon of Leicester.

To these thirteen *reformers* were entrusted the duty to compile the Book of Common Prayer, when our Church wrested herself from the base *servitude* which, for four hundred years, the Church of Rome had subjected her to.

When we find above the names of *Cranmer and Ridley*, surely we might be satisfied that, as they sealed their faith *with their blood in martyrdom*, so we need not fear to accept the doctrines that they have handed down to us, and believe that what we find in the Prayer Book were the doctrines held by our early reformers !

If any one doubts that the service I have quoted from our Prayer Book were the principles of those who compiled it, listen to the words of RIDLEY, THE MARTYR, just before he suffered.

When questioned by the three Roman Catholic Bishops, of Lincoln, Gloucester, and Bristol, and charged with affirming and teaching " That the true natural body of Christ, after the consecration of the Priest, *is not really present* in the sacrament of the altar. That in the sacrament of the altar remaineth *still the substance* of bread and wine," he answered, " Both you and I agree herein, that in the sacrament *is the very true and natural body and blood of Christ, even that which was born of the Virgin Mary, which ascended into heaven, which sitteth at the right hand of God the Father, which shall come from thence to judge the quick and the dead; only we differ in modo, in the way and manner* of being.

" I, being fully by God's word thereunto persuaded, confess Christ's natural body to be in the sacrament indeed, by spirit and grace ; because, that whosoever receiveth worthily that bread and wine, receiveth effectuously Christ's body, and drinketh His blood ––that is, he is made effectually partaker of His passion ; and you make *a grosser* kind of being, enclosing a natural, a lively, and a moving body, under the shape or form of bread and wine."

And again, when charged that he had publicly asserted : " That in the sacrament of the altar remaineth still the *substance* of bread and wine," he answered : " That in the sacrament is a *certain change*, whereby that bread which was, before common bread, is now made a lively representation of Christ's body ; and is *not only a figure*, but effectuously representeth His body." "Notwithstanding this sacramental mutation, which all the doctors confess, the true *substance* and nature of bread and wine *remaineth*."

Such was the answer of Ridley ; and the Bishop's charge is *to the same effect*—and let those who so loudly asserted at Salisbury that it was the Romish doctrine of transubstantiation, go to the dictionary again and learn the true meaning of the word.

This brings me to the meeting of Tuesday last ; when our member for North Wilts, Mr. Long, thus spoke : " They must examine for themselves the nature of that system, which was more and more increasing on every side ; they must settle, each man for himself, and each woman for herself, whether it was the authoritative doctrinal system of the Church of England. If, holding the Bible in one hand and the Book of Common Prayer in the other, and comparing with them the doctrines given out to them by certain ecclesiastical authorities and a vast number of the clergy, they were unable to reconcile them with those of the Bible and the Prayer Book, there devolved upon them a duty of protesting against the inculcation of those doctrines ; and not only of protesting against, but of practically opposing them."

Now, the honourable member had several ecclesiastical gentlemen around him, who took an active and most eloquent part in the proceedings of the day; and, supposing he had *the Bible in one hand and the Prayer Book in the other*, AND THEY WERE BOTH OPEN, he could have told the Rev. Talbot Greaves, of Weymouth, when he declaimed against, and *denied*, "that there was *any altar* in the Christian Church, *and consequently* NO PRIEST,"—that he differed from St. Paul, who said, in the thirteenth chapter of Hebrews, when he wished to convert the Jews to the Christian Faith ! "WE HAVE AN ALTAR," (in the Christian Church) "whereof they have no right to eat who serve the tabernacle." He could also have told him, from the Prayer-book, when the reverend gentleman was denying the power to absolve sins, and that he himself was a Priest, and Lord Osborne too, and the Rev. W. E. Pears ; that they had *each of them* sought *for Priest's orders* in the Church of England, and had received authority from the Bishop as follows:— " Receive the Holy Ghost for the office and work of a Priest in the Church of God, now committed unto thee by the imposition of our hands. *Whose sins thou dost forgive, they are forgiven; and whose sins thou dost retain, they are retained,*" &c. Again, he could have put them in remembrance, and also have derived information for himself, who had just said, "It was the Priest's power that they objected to ; because, if the clergy had granted to them the power of granting absolution—of remitting and retaining sin at pleasure—it followed as a logical necessity that they must have the confessional." He could have surprised a great many in that Assembly-room : he could have *rebuked the three clergymen who denied this power;* and, I should think, have been astonished at himself, if he had read from the service "for the visitation of the sick," *the absolution,* as follows :—

" Our Lord Jesus Christ, *who hath left power to His Church to absolve* all sinners who truly repent and believe in Him, of His great mercy forgive thee thine offences ; and, by His authority COMMITTED TO ME, I ABSOLVE THEE *from all thy sins,* in the name of the Father, and of the Son, and of the Holy Ghost." The rubric preceding this says: " Here shall the sick person be moved to make a special CONFESSION of his sins, if he feels his conscience troubled with any weighty matter; AFTER *which confession* the PRIEST shall *absolve him* (if he humbly and heartily desire it), after this sort."

I have *read* of some few clergymen who have denied that they were Priests ; but I never *heard* one till Tuesday last, when Mr. Greaves, of Weymouth, so eloquently declared they were no such thing !

Then, after hearing the three clergymen who spoke, *denying the real presence in the sacrament,* and having alluded to the same himself, Mr. Long could have turned to the Communion Service, and read—" Dearly beloved, on Sunday next I purpose, through

God's assistance, to administer to all such as shall be religiously and devoutly disposed, the most comfortable sacrament of THE BODY AND BLOOD OF CHRIST," &c. Then, in the Exhortation: " For, as the benefit is great, if with a true penitent heart and lively faith we receive that holy sacrament (for then we spiritually *eat the flesh of Christ and drink His blood,*" &c.). Then the prayer before Consecration—"Grant us, therefore, gracious Lord, *so to eat the flesh* of Thy dear Son, Jesus Christ, *and to drink His blood,*" &c. And, in the act of Consecration, " Hear us, O merciful Father, we most humbly beseech Thee, and grant that we *receiving* these Thy creatures of *bread and wine,* according to Thy Son our Saviour Jesus Christ's holy institution, in remembrance of His death and passion, may be *partakers* of His most blessed *body and blood,*" &c.

Now, all this service that I have quoted was compiled, with a few exceptions mentioned in the Bishop's charge, by the thirteen individuals I have enumerated : and they may justly be termed *our early reformers.* Would that all the members of the reformed Church had consented to receive the doctrines put forth by them, *as those of the Church of England ! But this was not the case.*

During the reign of Queen Mary, the reformers either suffered martyrdom or exile. Those who, to save their lives, went into exile, went over to Germany, and unfortunately fell in with Calvin and Knox, at Geneva, *imbibed their principles;* and the consequence was, on their return to England, on the accession of Queen Elizabeth, they came with opinions at moral variance with the principles of those EARLY REFORMERS who had compiled our Prayer Book : they caused *division and dissension in the Church* till the eleventh year of the Queen's reign, when many of them *having in vain attempted* TO ALTER *the Prayer Book,* proclaimed EPISCOPACY as anti-Christian, *and left the Church !*

Would that they had *all gone away :* that they had had the *honesty* to have left an Establishment, the principles of which, laid down by *Cranmer* and *Ridley,* they *would* not believe. But it was not so ; *a certain portion remained who feared the sin of schism,* but still would not conform to the ritual of the English Church. They have existed ever since ; *causing that division in the Church,* for the space of three hundred years, *against which* our Saviour so earnestly prayed in His last prayer on earth—in the seventeenth chapter of St. John !

Unfortunately, things are not altered at the present day : and we find the Rev. Lord S. G. Osborne, the Rev. Talbot Greaves, and the Rev. E. W. Pears, SUCCESSORS of those members of the Established Church who imbibed the Lutheran, Genevan, or *Low Church* doctrine, and still REMAINED within the pale of the Church. A great deal was said by the several speakers at Salisbury about Protestantism and the *Protestant* Church. How fearfully they *forget* what they really are! Mr. Long could have told them, with the Prayer Book opened, that every day they read the service, they were *obliged to say what the Apostles taught them: " I believe* in the HOLY CATHOLIC Church !" He could have shown them that the Council of Nice had instructed them to say, in the Nicene Creed: "And I believe in one *Catholic* and Apostolic Church." And he could have referred them to the Athanasian Creed, which says, "Whosoever will be saved, before all things *it is necessary* that he hold *the Catholic Faith*," &c.

I could fill columns more on this subject, and *will* if you wish it; but, for the present, time and space will not allow it. And I earnestly appeal to you, that you will not allow your *influence* and your *names* to be further handled as A LEVER for the use of a faction, to *hinder* our worthy Bishop from the manly, courageous, and truly Christian manner in which he has so single-handed come forward to teach what you and I should have been taught by the clergy "from our youth up until now."

There is one thing I would allude to in the Bishop's charge, which those who are so set against him *cannot see:* the beautiful allusion at pages 123, 124, to the great doctrine of *justification by faith*. Get his charge and read it throughout; look at it without prejudice; and look to the Scriptures (as the Bereans of old did), and see if *these things are so.*"

I remain, my brother Churchwardens,

Yours faithfully and respectfully,

J. A. WILLIAMS.

BAYDON, NORTH WILTS, *July* 30, 1867.

THE END.

GILBERT AND RIVINGTON, PRINTERS, ST. JOHN'S SQUARE, LONDON.

www.ingramcontent.com/pod-product-compliance
Lightning Source LLC
Chambersburg PA
CBHW031805090426
42739CB00008B/1176